MW01713824

TREASURES FROM PAUL'S LETTERS VOL. II

by
Anthony M. Coniaris

Sermons on the Sunday Epistle lessons as read in the Eastern Orthodox Church. Volume II covers the months of March through August.

Light and Life Publishing Company
P.O. Box 26421
Minneapolis, MN 55426-0421

Copyright © 1979
Anthony M. Coniaris
Library of Congress Card No. 78-56638

All rights reserved. No part of this book may be reproduced, stored in a retrieval system, or transmitted in any form or by any means, electronic, mechanical, photocopying, recording, or otherwise, without the written permission of Light and Life Publishing Company.

ISBN 1-0-937032-06-9

Table of Contents

Don't Be a Stumbling-block

Meatfare Sunday (I Corinthians 8:8-9:2)

"Only take care lest this liberty of yours somehow become a stumbling block to the weak" (I Cor. 8:9).

A blind man was noted for a lantern he always carried. People often asked, "What use is the lantern to you, since you are blind?" The blind man replied, "I do not carry it to prevent my stumbling over others, but to keep them from stumbling over me."

This has always been one of the great challenges of Christians: to make certain that no one stumbles because the faith we profess with our lips is so different from the faith we practice in our everyday living.

This is the great truth St. Paul emphasizes in today's Epistle lesson when he writes,

> "Only take care lest this liberty of yours somehow become a stumbling block to the weak. For if anyone sees you, a man of knowledge, at table in an idol's temple, might he not be encouraged, if his conscience is weak, to eat food offered to idols? And so by your knowledge, this weak man is destroyed, the brother for whom Christ died. Thus, sinning against your brethren and wound-

> ing their conscience when it is weak, you sin against Christ. Therefore, if food is a cause of my brother's falling, I will never eat meat, lest I cause my brother to fall" (I Cor. 8:8-13).

In I Corinthians 9:12 he says,

> ". . . we endure anything, rather than put an obstacle in the way of the gospel of Christ."

In Romans he says,

> "If your brother is being injured by what you eat, you are no longer walking in love. Do not let what you eat cause the ruin of one for whom Christ died . . . it is right not to eat meat or drink wine or do anything that makes your brother stumble" (Romans 14:15, 20-21).

The Issue at Hand

At that time the marketplace in Corinth was flooded with meat that had been sacrificed to idols. One party of intelligent Christians believed that since the idols or false gods to whom this meat had been sacrificed did not even exist, there was nothing wrong in buying the meat for use at home, or eating it in a public place.

The weak Christians, however, who had just been converted from paganism were scandalized by this. The meat—they felt—had been given over to the demons which had now somehow taken possession of it. If they ate this meat, the demons would somehow gain entrance into their bodies.

Paul's Advice

Thus, Paul's advice is not to wound the conscience of those who are weak. Take care lest you become a stumbling block to the weak. "If food is a cause of my brother's falling, I will never eat meat, lest I cause my brother to fall—the brother for whom Christ died."

In other words, the one who is more intelligent yields, just as on a lake or at sea, the bigger sailboat yields to the smaller one. Paul is suggesting that we act lovingly towards each other and not use our greater insight, our deeper knowledge, to do violence to people who may know less.

What Jesus Says

Of no sin does Jesus speak more severely than that of being the cause of sin to others. He condemns sternly those who put a stumbling-block in the way of others. The word for stumbling-block is the Greek word *skandalon,* the bait-stick in a trap, the trigger on which an animal stepped, and which snapped shut the jaws of the trap. Later it came to mean anything set in a man's path to trip him up, to lead him astray so as to ruin him. "Stumbling-blocks are bound to come but woe to the man by whom the temptation or stumbling-block comes" said Jesus (Matthew 18:7). It is a sin to ruin one's own life; it is doubly a sin to ruin the life of another. It is terrible enough to learn to sin; it is disastrous to teach another, to lead or cause him to sin. If any one causes another to sin, said Jesus, it would be better for him that a millstone were hanged about his neck and he were drowned in the depth of the sea.

Sad Examples

How many prodigals are kept out of the church today by the unlovely characters, by the holier-than-thou attitude of those who are within the church. Stumbling-blocks!

As a young man Ghandhi was searching for the truth. He was looking for a religion that would emancipate India from the wicked caste system. He came to the conclusion that Christianity held the right answer to India's grave problems.

But one Sunday Ghandhi went to a Christian church. An usher coldly confronted him at the door and said, "Sir, this church is only for Europeans." Deeply disillusioned, Ghandhi that day walked away from that church and from Christianity. How different India's history might have been if Christ-likeness had been displayed by that usher, who turned out to be, instead, a great stumbling-block.

The place where most of us are stumbling-blocks is at home. How many young people are there today who never darken the door of the Church because of parents who were always criticizing the church or the pastor? How many young men stay away from church on Sunday because of dad, who, on Sunday morning, either buried himself in the paper or was out playing golf? Where do boys get the idea that being a man is simply a matter of being able to smoke, drink, play poker, swear, tell a dirty joke? They certainly don't dream it up in a vacuum! They get it watching men, men they admire and respect, men like dad and his friends. Erik Erikson said once, "The most deadly of all possible sins is the mutilation of a child's spirit."

How wise, then, the blind man who carried a lantern not to prevent his stumbling over others, but to keep others from stumbling over him!

The story is told of a group of young people standing

on a street corner. When a well-dressed businessman walked by, one of the young people said, "There goes the founder of our city's atheists' club." Another young person objected, "What do you mean, atheists' club? He is the President of the Board of Trustees of St. Luke's Church?" Whereupon the first young person exclaimed, "He may be, but he is the most immoral and dishonest person I know. He turns me off completely. If that's what faith in God does to a person, I'd rather be an atheist."

No Man Is an Island

No one lives unto himself, says Paul. No man is an island. We are all bound up together. When I make a decision, it must be not only in terms of myself. I must consider also my weaker brothers or sisters for whom Christ died. I must try not to offend their conscience.

When the devil tempts me to think that what I do concerns me alone, may the Holy Spirit help me to remember the consequences, to remember the other people who will be affected by my action, to remember Christ, to remember God. When you and I fall, it is not an isolated fall, the whole Church of God falls with us. We are all bound up together in the one body of Christ. We cannot act in isolation. So, if nothing else keeps you from doing wrong, remember your wife, your children, your Christian friends, your Church. Remember the people to whom you belong. Remember Christ Who loved you and gave Himself for you.

Although it is an important job for the lantern to keep others from stumbling over us as in the case of the blind man, an even more important job is for the lantern to shine brightly, inspiring others and showing them the way to goodness and life.

Don't be a stumbling-block, but do go out of your way to be an inspiration to others. "Let your light so shine before men," said Jesus, "that they may see your good works and give glory to your Father in heaven." A person dedicated a book he wrote to his parents with these beautiful words: "To the memory of dad whose heart was as a little child's, and mother in whose face I saw God."

Not being a stumbling-block is good, but it is not enough. It is too negative. Go Beyond it. Be an inspiration to someone. Anybody can be an inspiration to somebody if his life is lived in Christ.

Put Away Jealousy, Put on Christ

Cheesefare Sunday (Romans 13:11-14:1)

"Let us conduct ourselves becomingly as in the day, not . . . in jealousy. But put on the Lord Jesus Christ, and make no provision for the flesh, to gratify its desires" (Rom. 13:13-14).

A legend tells of the devil crossing the Libyan Desert. There he met a number of his demons tempting a holy hermit. They tried to involve the hermit in sins of the flesh without success. He resisted all their temptations steadfastly. Finally, after watching their failure in disgust, the devil whispered to his demons, "What you do is too crude. Permit me one moment." Then the devil whispered to the holy man, "Have you heard the good news? Your brother has just been elected Bishop of Alexandria." The fable says, "Immediately a scowl of malignant jealousy clouded the serene face of the holy man." "That," said the devil to his crew, "is the sort of thing which I recommend."

It seems that the devil has been busy tempting us with jealousy and envy ever since the beginning of man.

When Cain and Abel brought their offerings to God, God accepted Abel's sacrifice and rejected Cain's. Cain was so jealous that he killed his brother. The world's first murder was born of jealousy.

Jacob made a beautiful coat for Joseph, his beloved son. "But when his brothers saw that their father loved him more than all his brothers, they hated him, and could not speak peacably to him" (Gen. 37:4). Because of jealousy they thought of killing Joseph, but instead sold him into slavery.

After David's victory over the Philistines, the women danced in the streets singing, "Saul has slain his thousands, and David his ten thousands" (I Sam. 18:7). Saul was so jealous he sought more than once to kill David.

When the older brother came in from the fields, he heard the sounds of a great celebration. Informed that it was a party to celebrate the return of his younger brother, he turned green with envy. " 'Lo,' he said to his father, 'these many years I have served you, and I never disobeyed your commands; yet you never gave me a kid, that I might make merry with my friends. But when this son of yours came, who has devoured your living with harlots, you killed for him the fatted calf!' " (Luke 15:29-30). Jealous, he refused to join the party.

" 'Do you want me to release to you the king of the Jews?' asked Pilate, knowing it was out of envy that the chief priests had handed Jesus over to him" (Mark 15:9, 10). It was envy that crucified our Lord!

A Great Sin of the Spirit

In the Epistle lesson today, Paul places jealousy in the same category as the sins of drunkenness, debauchery and licentiousness. "Let us conduct ourselves becomingly as in the day, not in reveling and drunkenness, not in debauchery and licentiousness, not in quarreling and jealousy" (Romans 13:13). The first sins he mentions are sins of the flesh; the last one—jealousy—is a sin of the spirit. The younger brother in the parable of the prodigal son sinned in the flesh—in drunkenness, debauchery, and licentiousness. The older brother sinned in the spirit—in jealousy. In the end, the one who sinned in the flesh was on the inside of the father's house, and the one who sinned in the spirit—in jealousy—was on the outside. Jealousy can close the doors of the Kingdom of God just as tightly as debauchery and licentiousness.

Of the sins of the spirit, the vice of envy and jealousy is near the top of the list.

Some of us may have seen logs caught on a rock in mid-stream and held up there, never reaching their destination. How many there are who are hung up on the rock of jealousy, and life flows past them.

"For while there is jealousy and quarreling among you, are you not worldly and behaving like ordinary men?" (I Cor. 3:3).

"Let us not become conceited, provoking and envying one another" (Gal. 5:26).

"At one time we too . . . lived in malice and envy, being hated and hating one another. But when the kindness and love of God our Savior appeared, he saved us" (Titus 3:3-5).

"Therefore, rid yourselves of all malice and all deceit, hypocrisy, jealousy, and slander of every kind" (I Peter 2:1).

Jealousy Distorts

Jealousy distorts and throws everything out of focus. A jealous husband or wife can make life miserable for himself and others by reading things that are not true into what people do. The result is a spreading misery. It is as malignant as a spreading cancer. "I'm on the road to recovery from a cancer—a mental cancer," said a woman who called her jealousy by its right name.

The envious person's attitude toward others is: "I don't want you to have what you have. If I can't have it, why should you?" How much of that rat-race called "keeping up with the Jones's" is nothing but envy! How much of our criticism of others is nothing but envy! How much of advertising is nothing but envy telling us: "If you buy this product, you'll be the envy of your friends."

There is an old story about an envious man. Looking at his neighbor's successes and achievements with envious eyes, begrudging him his lovely wife, his spacious home, his excellent position, and his new car, this man cried out one day, "If only I could be successful and rich! Then I would be happy!"

Suddenly an angel appeared and said, "I am here to grant your every wish—on one condition."

"Yes, yes," said the man eagerly, "What's that condition?"

"Just this," answered the angel. "Every time you get something, your neighbor across the street will get twice as much. If you get a million dollars, he will immediately get two million dollars."

A cloud came over the man's face. Already he had become envious of the two million dollars which the neighbor did not yet have. After some deep thought, he told the angel sadly, "I cannot take your offer. It would not be worth it. Why should my neighbor get double of everything I want to have? That would spoil everything." Sorrowfully, the angel left him stewing in his own juice.

The legend is not far fetched. We all have the urge to outdo the next man. There is nothing wrong with this *except* when it is born of envy.

There is a Greek story about a man who killed himself through envy. His fellow citizens had created a statue to one of their number who was a celebrated champion in the public games. But this man, a rival of the honored athlete, was so envious that he vowed that he would destroy the statue. Every night he went out into the darkness and chiseled at its base in an effort to undermine its foundation and make if fall. At last he succeeded. It did fall—but it fell on him. He died, a victim of his own envy.

HOW TO OVERCOME ENVY

A. Put On Christ

St. Paul offers us a way out of jealousy and envy. "Put on the Lord Jesus Christ," he says in the Epistle lesson. Put Him on every day through prayer and the reading of His word. Put on "the mind of Christ" (I Cor. 2:16) so that we think what He thinks, see what He sees, will what He wills. Every day put on His compassion, His kindness, lowliness, meekness, His patience, His forgiveness, and above all His love, which binds everything together in perfect harmony (Col. 3:12-14). Put on the Lord Jesus by receiving Him in Holy Communion. He will crowd out of life every envious and jealous thought. He will fill us with love—the love that is "patient and kind," the love which "does not envy, does not boast, and is not proud" (I Cor. 13:4).

B. Make No Provision for the Flesh

A second way of overcoming envy and jealousy offered by Paul in today's Epistle lesson is found in the words, "Make no provision for the flesh to satisfy its desires" (Rom. 13:14). Kill your spiritual enemies by starvation, he says. Destroy them by neglect. Make no provision for them. Starve them to death. Where there is no wood, the fire goes out. Deny the fuel and you exhaust the flame. We must confess our envy and jealousy to Christ. We must pray to be baptized by Christ's love. We must look at the enviable one in our Master's presence, and he will become to us the lovable one. Envy is asphyxiated in the atmosphere of prayer. In prayer there is no provision for jealousy or envy.

C. Thankfulness

Destroy these enemies by living in an atmosphere of prayer *and thankfulness.* When a person is thankful, he is concentrating on what he has, rather than on what he doesn't have. When a person is thankful he is looking up to God, not around him at the possessions of others. When a person is thankful, he is counting his blessings, not his failures. When a person is thankful, he is acknowledging the grace of God, not the avarice, stinginess and greed of people.

The cancer of jealousy cannot survive in an atmosphere of prayer, thankfulness and love where Christ is present.

"Let us conduct ourselves as in the day, not . . . in jealousy. But put on the Lord Jesus Christ, and make no provision for the flesh, to gratify its desires" (Rom. 13:13-14).

PRAYER

O Christ, forgive my envy and heal my jealous heart. Amen.

Greater Wealth Than the Treasures of Egypt

The First Sunday of Lent (Hebrews 11:21-26; 32-40)

"He considered abuse suffered for the Christ greater wealth than the treasures of Egypt, for he looked to the reward" (Hebrews 11:26).

Adopted by the Pharoah's daughter, Moses had been brought up in great luxury in Egypt. He was heir to a kingdom. But he had never forgotten his people. And the day came when he decided to join his people, the downtrodden Israelites. To do so, he left behind the riches and ease and comfort and royalty he might have had.

Like Christ Who gave up His heavenly glory for the suffering inflicted by man, Moses gave up all earthly glory for the sake of the people of God. He chose the loyalty that led to suffering rather than the ease which led to glory on earth. He chose to suffer for the right than enjoy luxury with the wrong. He knew that the prizes earth had to offer were of no comparison when placed alongside the ultimate reward of God. So the writer of Hebrews says, "He considered abuse suffered for the Christ greater wealth than the treasures of Egypt, for he looked to the reward" (Hebrews 11:26).

The Real Treasures in Life

One of the marks of true wisdom is to be able to discern the real treasures in life; the ones that last and bring true contentment. So many of us wear ourselves out for treasures that turn out to be no treasures at all.

> He used his health
> To store up wealth . . .
> Then spent his wealth
> To get back health
> And only got a grave.

There are people who start out to make money and end up with money making them something they never expected to be. Dr. Karl Meninger tells of treating patients whose lives were choked by the sin of greed. He tells of one, a millionaire, who was brought by relatives for treatment after he had tried suicide. Life, he said, no longer held anything of interest to him. "And I haven't the slightest idea," he said, "what to do with all my money. I don't need it all, but I can't bear to give any away."

"So you decide to kill yourself," asked Dr. Meninger, "in order to get away from it?"

"Well, what else can I do?" he replied.

Dr. Menninger suggested to him many good things he could do with his money. The millionaire said he would think about it, but did nothing. He died prematurely a few years later to the satisfaction of his heirs who, says Dr. Menninger, "were not yet in his predicament, although they suffered from the same 'disease.' "

God had given Moses the ability to discern between true treasures and false ones. "He considered abuse suffered for Christ greater wealth than the treasures of

Egypt, for he looked to the reward" (Hebrews 11:26).

Snails or Heaven?

There is a story based on an old legend about a beautiful swan that flew down from the sky to converse with a crane he saw wading in a shallow stream looking for snails.

"Where did you come from?" inquired the crane.

"I came from heaven," replied the swan.

"And where is that?" asked the other bird.

"Have you never heard of heaven with its streets of gold, its gates of pearl, and its river of life clear as crystal?"

"No," said the crane.

Then in eloquent terms the swan described the eternal city with its resplendent joy. The crane was not at all interested, but asked, "Are there any snails there?"

"No, of course not," was the reply.

"Then you can have your heaven," said the other bird as it continued its search along the slimy banks of the stream. "I want snails!"

How many there are who turn their backs on God and heaven and the true treasures of life because they have made snails their great treasure in life. Not so Moses! "He considered abuse suffered for the Christ greater than the treasures of Egypt, for he looked to the reward" (Hebrews 11:26).

The Unsearchable Riches of Christ

If it were announced today that all our paper money would be worthless tomorrow, we would all be anxious to exchange it quickly for things of more permanent value. Actually all our money, houses and lands, will one day be worthless. So Jesus asks us to exchange them now for "treasures in heaven," or for what St. Paul calls "the unsearchable riches of Christ" (Eph. 3:8).

Jesus comes to a man living for snails and He says, "May I come in?" If He is allowed to enter and stay, He will bring the treasures of heaven to that man and teach him that the be-all and end-all of life is not just to get rich but to usc the riches God gives us to enrich the world.

"He considered abuse suffered for the Christ greater wealth than the treasures of Egypt, for he looked to the reward" (Hebrews 11:26).

Wiped Out?

A few years ago a businessman lost his entire fortune. He went to his home and in utter despair flung himself down in the big chair. "Honey," he said to his wife, "we are ruined—wiped out!"

The wife replied, "You have me left. Together we will earn another fortune."

His aged mother came and, placing a trembling hand on her son's head, said, "My son, you have God left."

His little girl of nine years climbed up on the arm of the chair, put her arms about his neck, and said, "Daddy, you have me left."

The disconsolate man sprang to his feet, saying, "I am a millionaire! I am rich in the things that cannot be taken away!"

This story brings to memory a disastrous fire that left a man's business in smoldering ruins. Over the charred debris, he placed a large sign with these words: Everything lost except wife, children, hope, and faith in God. Business will be resumed as usual soon."

What Money Cannot Buy

George Lorimer said once, "It's good to have money and the things money can buy. It's good, too, to check up once in a while and make sure you haven't lost the things money can't buy."

"He considered abuse suffered for the Christ greater wealth than the treasures of Egypt, for he looked to the reward" (Hebrews 11:26).

I can find no better words with which to conclude than those of St. Paul in I Timothy 6:17-19:

"As for the rich in this world, charge them not to be haughty, nor to set their hopes on uncertain riches but on God who richly furnishes us with everything to enjoy. They are to do good, to be rich in good deeds, liberal and generous, thus laying up for themselves a good foundation for the future, so that they may take hold of the life which is life indeed."

PRAYER

Precious Lord, as did Moses, may we, too,
seek that wealth which is greater than the
treasures of Egypt—the wealth that is to be found in
loving and serving You in all that we do.
Amen.

"Are They Not Ministering Spirits?"

Second Sunday of Lent (Hebrews 1:10-2:4)

"Are they not all ministering spirits sent forth to serve, for the sake of those who are to obtain salvation?" (Hebrews 1:14).

At a town meeting in the South, the local Episcopal clergyman opposed a political boss named Sam. The result was that a proposal Sam made was defeated. Sam didn't like this and he announced publicly that he was going to kill the minister. Friends came to the minister and said, "We had better walk home with you tonight, because it is a lonely walk, and Sam will do what he said. You have to pass that dark wood lot."

The minister refused protection and walked home alone, right through the dark wood lot and nothing happened to him.

A few years later Sam, on his death bed, sent for this same minister. "Reverend, I meant to kill you that night," he said. "I was in the woods with a club, all ready to knock your brains out."

"Sam, why didn't you do it?" the minister asked.

"What do you mean, why didn't I do it? Who were those two big men with you?"

"There were no big men with me," the minister replied.

"Oh, yes, there were," said Sam. "I saw them."

The clergyman then realized that God had sent His angels to protect him.

Delivered By God's Angels

John G. Paton, a missionary to the New Hebrides Islands, tells a thrilling story about the protective care of angels. Hostile natives surrounded his mission one night, intent on burning the Patons out and killing them.

All through that terror-filled night Paton and his wife prayed that God would deliver them. When daylight came, they were amazed to see the attackers unaccountably pick up and leave. The Patons offered a prayer of thanks to God for delivering them.

A year later, the chief of the tribe was converted to Christ. Remembering what had happened, Paton asked the chief what had kept him and his men from burning down the house and killing them. The chief replied in surprise, "Who were all those men you had with you there?"

The missionary answered, "There were no men there; just my wife and I."

The chief insisted that they had seen many men standing guard—hundreds of big men in shining garments with drawn swords in their hands. They circled the mission so that the natives were afraid to attack. Only then did Paton realize that God had sent His angels to protect them.

Miraculous Rescue

During World War II, Captain Eddie Rickenbacker

was shot down over the Pacific Ocean. For weeks nothing was heard of him. The newspapers reported his disappearance and across the country thousands of people prayed. Mayor Laguardia asked the whole City of New York to pray for him.

Then he was found and rescued from a raft. The papers headlined the story. In an article, Rickenbacker himself told what had happened. "And this part I would hesitate to tell," he wrote, "except that there were six witnesses who saw it with me."

"A gull came out of nowhere and lighted on my head. I reached up my hand very gently. I killed him and then we divided him equally among us. We ate every bit, even the little bones. Nothing ever tasted so good." The gull saved the lives of Rickenbacker and his companions.

Years later, when he was asked how he could account for the gull, he replied, "I have no explanation except that God sent one of His angels to rescue us."

Peter's Deliverance

In the twelfth chapter of the Book of Acts we read the dramatic story of Peter's deliverance from prison:

". . . Peter was sleeping between two soldiers, bound with two chains, and sentries before the door were guarding the prison; and behold, an angel of the Lord appeared, and a light shone in the cell; and he struck Peter on the side and woke him, saying, 'Get up quickly.' And the chains fell off his hands. And the angel said to him, 'Dress yourself and put on your sandals.' And he did so. And he said to him, wrap your mantle around you and follow me.' And he went out and followed him; he did not know that what was done by the angel was real, but thought he was seeing a vision. When they had passed the first and the second guard, they came to the iron gates leading into the city. It opened to them of its own accord, and they went out and passed on through one street; and immediately the angel left him. And Peter came to himself, and said, 'Now I am sure that the Lord has sent His angel and rescued me from the hand of Herod . . .' " (Acts 12:6-11).

Speaking of angels the writer of Hebrews says in the Epistle lesson today: "Are they not all ministering spirits sent forth to serve, for the sake of those who are to obtain salvation?" (Hebrews 1:14).

Angels? Why do they fly? asked someone. G. K Chesterton replied, "They fly because they take themselves lightly." But as Christians we do not take them lightly. So let's examine first:

Who Are the Angels?

A long, long time ago, long before God made Adam and Eve, even before He made the sun and the moon and the stars, God made some beings, or people without bodies to live with Him in heaven.

They are called angels.

Since they have no bodies, we cannot see the angels or talk with them, but they see us. Some of them are present with us right now. The angels are "ministering spirits." In other words they are God's helpers. In fact, God has asked at least one angel to be a special helper to each one of us—a guardian angel (Matthew 18:10). One of the functions of angels is to guard and protect. The Greek word "angelos" means messenger. The angels are also God's messengers. If we place the Greek word "ev" which means "good," before "angel," we have the word *evangel,*i.e., a messenger who brings good news. The angels are the messengers of God's good news.

Their Ministry in the Bible

It was an angel who appeared to the Virgin Mary to tell her the greatest good news this world has ever heard: that the Lord Jesus was to be born and that she was going to be His mother. It was a great choir of angels that came to the shepherds on the hillside that first Christmas, praising God and announcing that the Lord Jesus was born in Bethlehem. It was an angel who warned Joseph to take Mary and the Child and flee into Egypt to escape the wrath of Herod. Angels were with Jesus in the wilderness to comfort Him when He was tempted. They were with Him in the agony of Gethsemane just before His crucifixion to strengthen Him. When Peter drew his sword to ward off Christ's arrest, the Master reminded him that, if He wanted, He might have "more than 12 legions of angels" to assist Him. A legion numbered 6,000 men. It was an angel who rolled the huge stone away from Christ's tomb. It was an angel who on Resurrection morning announced to the disciples: "He is risen. He is not here!" It was with a company of angels that Jesus ascended into heaven—the same angels who will accompany Him when He comes back to take control of the human race and to establish His kingdom.

The Meaning of Angels

The existence of angels tells us that God is constantly and secretly intervening in the lives of His children to guide, comfort, strengthen and protect them. Angels tell us that this is not a closed universe but always open to God's loving, caring intervention. Angels tell us that this universe is not just materialistic; there is more than just materialism; there is spirit, there is God, there are His ministering angels. Angels tell us that it is not just the devil who exists, going about "as a roaring lion, seeking some one to devour" (I Peter 5:8). There are also God's angels to protect us along the way. People today are looking for assurance that the devil is not in control. They do not have to be convinced anymore that there is a devil. They know it! They have seen him in the lives of others and sometimes in their own life. What they want to know is: Is that all there is? No! There are angels, God's "ministering spirits sent forth to serve for the sake of those who are to obtain salvation."

In the Eastern Orthodox Church we commemorate the holy angels every year on the Feast Day of the Archangel Michael on November 8. In addition, the second day every week, Monday, is dedicated to the memory of the holy angels. There are numerous references to the presence of the angels in the Divine Liturgy. With them we stand before God's throne and sing their hymn of praise, "Holy, holy, holy . . ."

How Do They Come to Us?

Before we conclude let us ask a very relevant question: what form do angels take today? How do they come to us?

As in days of old, angels come to us in many ways. One way is through the Word of God, the Holy Bible. The Bible is God's word to us today. It is help from beyond. It is a strengthening and comforting angel if we read it daily and keep its words in our minds and hearts. Take a promise from God's Word with you every day, commit it to memory, meditate on it, pray it, and see if it doesn't become a strengthening angel to you.

Secondly, a fellow-creature can be an angel. How often we hear it said, "You have been an angel of God to me." A person died once and went to heaven. St. Peter asked him, "What would you like to be up here?" The man thought and said, "An angel." St. Peter asked, "What sort of experience have you had in this field?"

I never saw an angel like they show on
  Christmas things,
Who stand so tall and handsome with
  mighty folded wings.
No, I never saw that kind of one, and yet
  I'm sure it's true
That there are angels hard at work
  for folks like me and you.

I've seen them come up to the door with
  cake and soup and such,
I've seen them help where folks were sick,
  and help so very much.
No, I've never seen a tall one with
  wings and halo, too—
But helpful deeds and kindly words
  show angels must be true.

—Dr. Frederick L. Brown

A clergyman was calling in his parish one day. He knocked on a door and a woman's voice called out: "Is that you, Angel?"

"No," came the minister's prompt reply, "but I'm from the same department."

Aren't we all called to be from the same department?

When asked the character in history he envied

most, the one he would have asked to be if he could have been given his choice, one person said he would have liked to have been the angel in the garden who strengthened Jesus in His agony. But we have our Lord's word that we can indeed be that angel by being sensitive to the needs of others, by caring, by listening, by praying, by standing with people who hurt, by a caring word, by helping lift a heavy load. "As you did it to one of the least of these My brethren, you did it to Me," said Jesus.

Aren't there "angel" mothers? "angel" fathers? "angel" friends? who help us out of difficult situations? who fill us with hope? who guide us in the ways of righteousness and lead us to God?

It Is Jesus!

It was a dark night. A fierce storm was raging on Lake Galilee. The winds were a howling gale. Caught in their boat on the lake, the disciples were sure they would never live to see the light of morning. Peering into the darkness, they thought they saw something moving swiftly toward them across the waters. At first they imagined it was a ghost, then an angel, then suddenly there came a great shout from Peter—"It's the Master! It's Jesus!" The Lord of angels—Jesus Himself—had appeared on that terrible night to bring comfort and strength to His helpless disciples. Often the angel who appears is none other than the Lord Jesus Himself. In a sense, it is always Christ Who appears through His angels. After all, whose angels are they? Who sends them? Whom do they serve? Whether it be a real angel such as delivered the Episcopal clergyman, Paton, Rickenbacker, Peter, and countless others; or whether it be a word from the Bible or just a friend whose love and concern make him an angel to us in time of need—it is always Christ: His love, His care, His concern that stand behind each angel who comes to us. So there is nothing more important in life than that we pray constantly for the real presence of the living Christ in our everyday lives.

PRAYER

Thank you, Lord, for your love, protection and guidance through Your angels. As Your love abides in us help us, too, to be Your ministering angels of mercy to those about us. Amen.

Let Us Draw Near

Third Sunday of Lent (Hebrews 4:14-5:6)

"Let us then with confidence draw near to the throne of grace, that we may receive mercy and find grace to help in time of need" (Hebrews 4:16).

There are those who believe that the whole essence of the Letter to the Hebrews is captured by this one text: "Let us draw near to the throne of grace." Its central idea is that it has now become possible through Jesus Christ to approach God freely.

It was not always so. The tragedy of the Garden of Eden was that Adam and Eve lost God. They ran away from Him. They separated themselves from Him. A great wall was erected between God and man—the wall of man's sin and separation.

It was not possible for man to "draw near to the throne of grace." In the Old Testament temple a great curtain separated the Holy of Holies from the people. No man could enter the Holy of Holies but the high priest—and he only once a year on the Day of Atonement. And he was not to linger too long in that holiness "lest he put Israel in terror."

There were tiny bells along the hem of Aaron's robe to announce his every movement as he ministered in the

Holy of Holies (Exodus 28:33-35). (Orthodox bishops to this day wear these bells on their robes). Those outside would know if Aaron had died in God's presence by the absence of the tinkling sound. For no man could see God and live. Moses heard God say: "You cannot see my face; for no man shall see me and live" (Exodus 33:20). God's name was so holy that it was forbidden for the Jew to use it. If there was one word to describe God in the Old Testament, it would be the word *unapproachable.*

God's Great Plan

God's great plan of redemption in Christ had one supreme purpose—to break down the barrier of sin which made God so unapproachable, to return man to God. The cross which forgave man's sin and guilt, was God's way of removing the barrier that separated man from Him, in order that man might again live with God and walk with Him as in the Garden of Eden.

Every year on the Third Sunday of Lent Orthodox Christians have a ceremony of the flowering of the cross. Garden flowers are placed on and around the cross to signify that what was once an object of execution has now become a door that leads us into God's presence producing new life in sublime beauty and fragrance. The cross is presented to us in the middle of Lent as a reminder of God's having drawn near to us in Christ.

The Latin word for priest is *pontifex*, which means literally a bridge-builder. The essence of the Gospel in the Letter to the Hebrews is that Jesus Christ is for us the bridge into the presence of God. He is the *archegos* of our faith (Hebrews 12:2)—the pioneer who blazes the way into the presence of God that we may follow. He is the *prodromos* (Hebrews 6:20)—the scout who went on ahead to see that it was safe for the main body to follow. In Christ we now have access to the presence of God. At his death the curtain separating man from the Holy of Holies was torn from top to bottom. God is now exposed, revealed, approachable.

"Since then we have a great high priest who has passed through the heavens, Jesus, the Son of God, let us hold fast our confession . . . Let us then with confidence draw near to the throne of grace, that we may receive mercy and find grace to help in time of need" (Hebrews 4:14, 16).

The Approachable God

God in Christ is approachable. He was approachable to the Samaritan woman at the well; He was approachable to the man with the withered hand, to the deaf, to the lame; He was approachable to the blind beggar who called out to Him from the gutter of a street, to the leper who was afraid to come near Him, to the penitent thief who died next to Him on the cross. Approachable!

"Let us then with confidence draw near to the throne of grace, that we may receive mercy and find grace to help in time of need" (Hebrews 4:16).

The entire ministry of Christ on earth was a testimony to the fact that He is approachable. No matter how great our need, no matter how deep our sorrow, no matter how heavy our burden, no matter how black our sins, no matter how hopeless our situation, He is always approachable. Over His life, then and now, stand the glorious words, "Come unto me all ye that labor and are heavy laden and I will give you rest" (Matt. 11:28). To emphasize its reality, the Savior adds, "And him that cometh to me I will in no wise cast out."

He is approachable today:

approachable in our sorrow to dry our tears;
approachable in death to sustain us with the hope of everlasting life;
approachable in our weakness to strengthen us with His divine grace;
approachable in our confusion to guide us to the abundant life;
approachable in our hunger and thirst after righteousness to satisfy us with the bread of life;
approachable in our sins to grant us a forgiveness that will put song in our hearts.

"Let us then with confidence draw near to the throne of grace, that we may receive mercy and find grace to help in time of need."

"Draw near to God and He will draw near to you" (James 4:8).

Draw Near!

Draw Near!

Each morning when I wake, I say,
"I place my hand in God's today."
I know He'll walk close by my side
my ever wandering step to guide.
He leads me with the tenderest care
when paths are dark and I despair.
No need for me to understand
If I but hold fast to His hand.
My hand in His! No surer way
To walk in safety through each day.
By His great bounty I am fed
Warmed by His love, and comforted.

When at day's end I seek my rest
And realize how much I'm blessed
My heart pours out to Him, and then,
I place my hands in God's again.

Draw near! Jesus has no favorites only intimates who like the Apostle John share with Him their love and devotion (John 13:23). "I no longer call you slaves . . . I have called you friends" (John 15:15). Jesus offers an intimacy with God which was impossible before His coming.

Draw near!

In the 17th century a bishop named Francois de Fenelon wrote these instructive words regarding our relationship with the Lord: "Tell Him all that is in your heart like one who unloads his pent-up feelings to a dear friend. People who have no secrets from each other never want for subjects on which to converse. They do not struggle for something to say, they just talk out of the abundance of their love. Blessed are they who attain to such familiar, unreserved intercourse with Him."

Draw near!

H. K. Downie tells about a large newspaper that offered a substantial amount of cash for the best answer to the question, "What is the shortest way to London?" The entry which won the prize was: "The shortest way to London is good company!" Says Downie, "All travelers know how true that answer is. Loving companionship shortens any journey, however long. Time flies because of the pleasure of fellowship. The journey to Heaven, though often accompanied by trials, is also shortened and made easier when Jesus Christ is our traveling companion."

Draw near to this Divine Friend!

"Since We Have Jesus . . . "

"Since we have . . . Jesus . . . let us hold fast our confession . . . Let us with confidence draw near to the throne of grace . . . " We can hold fast our faith and draw near to the throne of grace *because we have Jesus*! This is the crux! This is the pillar on which we rest! We have Jesus Who stands at the mercy-seat as our Savior, our merciful and faithful High Priest Who gave His life to forgive our sins. He waits to give us pardon and grace, strength and power for life's complexities. How can we not draw near to such a loving Savior and faithful High Priest?

Connected to Power

A certain bishop once said, "Nothing gets anywhere until it is connected. A horse never pulls until it is harnessed. A Niagara never produces power until it is tunneled. Steam never drives anything until it is channeled. No human life ever produces until it is connected with the power of God."

Draw near to Him through prayer. The purpose of prayer is to connect our life to God so that His love and power may flow through us into the lives of others around us.

Draw near to Him through Holy Communion. "With the fear of God, with faith and with love *let us draw near*" is the invitation we hear in every liturgy. "Let us with faith and longing *draw near* that we may become partakers of life everlasting," says the hymn at the moment of the Great Entry in the Liturgy of the Presanctified Gifts. Draw near to the throne of grace in every liturgy. Ascend with Christ to the throne of that grace. Receive Him Who is the Bread of Life and return to your worldly tasks with new wisdom and greater power.

Draw near to him through faith, through repentance, through love.

What is Lent if not a time to draw near to Him?

When You Are Sorely Troubled

When you are sorely troubled by what is happening to you, when your faith is troubled, when God seems far away and there is no peace in your heart, *draw near*!

When you feel your inner world is going to pieces, *draw near*!

When you lack the strength to resist temptation, *draw near*!

When your principles and ideals—the standards by which you live—are being undermined and destroyed on all sides, *draw near*!

When the storms of life roar about you, *draw near*!

Christ has opened a new and living way to God. The veil is rent. The wall is down. We have access to grace, access to the Father, access to the Holy Spirit, access to power, access to forgiveness, access to God's mercy, and Christ is our High Priest to represent us in the Holy Place of God's throne. So let us draw near not tomorrow but today. For tomorrow is not ours. Tomorrow may never come. Tomorrow may be too late. "Seek ye the Lord while he may be found," says that prophet, "call ye upon him while he is near. Let the wicked forsake his way and the unrighteous man his thoughts; and let him return unto the Lord and he will have mercy upon him and to our God for He will abundantly pardon" (Isaiah 55:6-7).

PRAYER

Lord, if You seem far removed from us, it is because we have drawn away from You. Help us to draw near to You that we may receive mercy and find grace to help in time of need. Amen.

On Being Patient

Fourth Sunday of Lent (Hebrews 6:13-20)

"And thus Abraham, having patiently endured, obtained the promise" (Hebrews 6:15).

Customers in a supermarket were paying more and more attention to a man who was pushing a cart which contained a screaming baby. The man repeated softly: "Don't get excited, Albert; don't scream, Albert; don't yell, Albert; keep calm, Albert; be patient, Albert."

A woman finally stepped up to the man and said, "You certainly are to be commended for being so patient with your son Albert."

The man stopped and said: "Lady, I'm Albert."

Patience is a great virture. "If I have ever made any valuable discoveries," said Sir Isaac Newton, "it has been owing more to patient attention than to any other talent." It is about this virtue of patience that the Epistle lesson speaks today when it says, "And thus Abraham, having patiently endured, obtained the promise" (Hebrews 6:15). God had promised to multiply the seed of Abraham. But Abraham had to exercise patience before he received the promise. It was not until twenty-five years after God's promise that his son Isaac was born. Abraham was old; Sarah was barren; but Abraham waited patiently, trusting in the promise of God.

Imagine waiting twenty-five years for God to fulfill a promise. That is patience! Contrast this with the mood today which is for instant everything. Instant sound through the transistor radio. Instant destruction through A-bombs. Instant "turning on" through drugs. Instant direct-dialing to any spot in the world. Instant photographs. Instant riches. Instant breakfast. Instant soup. Instant pain relievers. Instant tranquilizers. Instant sex. Instant abortion. Instant divorce. Instant suicide.

So people ask: Why not instant prayer? Why wait twenty-five years, as Abraham did, for an answer to prayer? Why not right now?

When a father asked a college president for an instant education for his son who did not want to spend four whole years in college, he received the reply: "Certainly, I believe I can arrange for that. Of course, it all depends on what you want to make of your boy. When God wants to make an oak tree, He takes a hundred years. When he wants to make a squash, He takes only two months."

What Is Patience?

Patience is love at work.

Patience is a mother who loves her small child even after he has spilled a glass of milk on himself and the clean tablecloth.

Patience is a father teaching his son how to drive an automobile without getting angry at him for his every wrong move.

Patience is the ability to count down before blasting off.

Patience is the man in his wheelchair and the woman in her walker thanking God for their blessings and bearing their hardships with a smile.

Patience is a child learning to walk, falling again and again, yet trying, improving, until one day he walks without falling.

Patience is Abraham waiting twenty-five years for God to fulfill His promise.

Patience is perservering five minutes longer than your opponent, digging three feet deeper in your search for oil, fighting one more round, waiting one day longer before calling it quits. Zane Grey didn't sell a single story during his first five years of writing, but he kept on.

Patience is what God must have in dealing with us every day.

Patience is the whole Old Testament waiting for the coming of the Messiah.

Patience is waiting on the Lord, "waiting for the promise of the Father," "waiting for the revealing of our Lord Jesus Christ," "waiting for adoption as sons, the redemption of our bodies."

Patience is the testimony of a little old lady who sold flowers on the street: "When Jesus was crucified on Good Friday, that was the worst day for the whole world. And when I get troubles I remember that. Yet only three days later came Easter. So when I get troubles I've learned to give God a chance to help. I wait three days."

Patience is waiting for someone. For the Christian, it is waiting for Jesus Who will appear to take us unto Himself, to usher in the fulness of His Kingdom, at which time there will be no more need of patience.

Patience is not inactivity. Patience hustles while it waits. It is dynamic. It bears things because it knows that God is in control, that He has a plan for my life. Patience is waiting and cooperating with God as He works out His plan for my life.

Patience is the quality which keeps a man on his feet with his face to the wind, transforming the hardest trial into glory because beyond the pain it sees the goal.

Patience with Ourselves

How much we need to be patient with ourselves! Patient with our failures and disappointments, never yielding to despair or self-pity; patient enough to rise again, even when we are bowed down with shame; patient enough not to give up on ourselves; patient enough to ask God to be patient with us; patient enough to begin again, this time with a humbler spirit, leaning more firmly on Christ.

Patience with Others

How much we need to be patient not only with ourselves but also with others! If we are having so many problems with ourselves, imagine how terribly others must be suffering. If only we could see their invisible wounds, how patient we would be.

How impatient we are with our children! When a son behaves childishly at the age of five, we ask, "Why don't you act like a big boy?" Why should he behave like a big boy when he's only five? Did his Creator intend him to be a big boy at five years of age? Why should he act like an adult, or an adolescent, or a ten-year-old when he is only five? I like the well-known saying: "Be patient with me, dad, God isn't finished with me yet."

How patient we need to be with the way some people treat us. "An insult is like mud," someone said, "it will brush off much better when it is dry." In dealing with insults, waiting for things to cool off is not only patience but also wisdom.

God's Patience with Us

The supreme example of patience is God. Jesus told a parable of a farmer who planted a fig tree. Three years he cultivated it, but it produced no fruit. He was ready to cut it down and burn it when the vinedresser, who represents God, said, "Let it alone, sir, this year also, till I dig about it and put on manure. And if it bears fruit next year, well and good; but if not, you can cut it down" (Luke 13:8-9). Is not this a picture of God's patience with each one of us, always giving us another chance, another year, another opportunity to repent, to return, to bear fruit for Him? Shall we allow that time to run out?

In Mark 12:1-11, Jesus tells another parable of the marvelous patience of God. The Lord of the vineyard sends first one servant, and he is beaten; then a second, and he is stoned; then a third, and he is killed; and then "many others." Then, instead of giving up, He sends His only beloved son saying, "They will reverence my Son." But they killed Him too. God's marvelous patience, sending one prophet after another, pleading in voice after voice, hoping that some day at long last His people would listen and repent. But this is not just the story of Israel. It is the story of how God has dealt with your life and mine. Having given His only Son for us, having done all He can, He waits patiently for us to turn to Him.

"If I were God," someone said, "and the world had treated me as it has treated Him, I would kick the wretched thing to pieces." But not God. His patience endures.

In delivering a lecture against Christ and the Bible, Robert Ingersoll, the atheist, dramatically took out his watch and said, "I'll give God a chance to prove that He exists and is almighty. I challenge Him to strike me dead within five minutes." The five minutes passed and Ingersoll said laughingly, "See! There is no God. I am still very much alive."

After the lecture, a young man said to a Christian lady, "Well, Ingersoll certainly proved something tonight!" Her reply was memorable. "Yes he did," she said. "He demonstrated that even the most defiant sinner cannot exhaust the patience of God in just five minutes."

The famous New England preacher, Phillips Brooks, looked deeply troubled one day. A friend asked him, "What's the trouble, Dr. Brooks?" "The trouble is," Brooks replied, "that I'm in a hurry—but God isn't."

Is not this one of our chief troubles today: we are in a hurry when God is not? The result is that our gears do not mesh with God's. We go fast. He goes slow. We strip our gears. We wear out and fall apart.

How to Gain Patience

Rudyard Kipling wrote, "If you can wait, and not be tired by waiting . . . you'll be a man, my son." It is so easy to tire by waiting. How does one gain patience? How does one persevere in it?

1. "We rejoice in our suffering, knowing that suffering produces patience" (Rom. 5:3). Patience does not

come from a prescription or a pill. It comes from suffering. A certain woman prayed for patience. She complained that while she prayed for patience, all she seemed to get was trouble. "The Lord is sending you trouble in order to produce patience in you," was the reply. "Suffering produces patience." So, the next time we face frustration, whether large or small, let's say to the Lord, "Thank you, Lord, for another opportunity to learn patience."

2. Patience is not a human achievement. It is a fruit of the Holy Spirit within us (Gal. 5:22). We must pray for it. It is a virtue that we receive when we live in Christ. If Shakespeare were in us, what poetry we could write. If Beethoven were in us, what music we could compose. If Christ were in us, what a life we could live! But there is no if about it. You cannot have an indwelling Shakespeare or Beethoven, but you can have an indwelling Christ, which means that in and through His power, you can have patience.

3. A doctor was once asked by a patient who had a serious accident: "Doctor, how long will I have to lie here in this hospital?" The doctor replied, "Only one day at a time." The answer taught the patient a precious lesson. All of life is lived one day at a time. With each day comes God's love and God's strength to bear the heaviest burden.

"They who wait upon the Lord shall renew their strength, they shall mount up with wings as eagles, they shall run and not be weary, they shall walk and not faint" (Is. 40:31).

PRAYER

Our patience, dear Lord, is nothing but waiting on

You, playing life according to Your game plan and giving You time to work out the final results. So we find delight in the words of the Psalmist: "I wait for the Lord, my soul waits, and in his Word I hope; my soul waits for the Lord more than watchmen for the morning" (Ps. 110:5-6). Amen.

That Inner Voice

Fifth Sunday of Lent (Hebrews 9:11-14)

" . . . how much more should the blood of Christ purify your conscience" (Hebrews 9:14).

A teacher was admonishing a high school boy for coming in late to class; "Don't you ever listen to the voice of conscience?" he asked. After a moment's hesitation the boy replied: "I don't think so—what channel is it on?"

We read in the Epistle lesson today: " . . . how much more shall the blood of Christ . . . purify your conscience."

What is that inner voice in each of us called conscience? How did it get there? Is there anyone behind it? What is its purpose? Why does it have the power to make man's life on earth a veritable heaven or hell?

St. Paul writes in Romans 2:14-16, "When the Gentiles who have not the law do by nature what the law requires, they are a law themselves, even though they do not have the law. They show that what the law requires is written on their hearts, while their conscience also bears witness . . . "

For St. Paul the world was divided into two classes of people: (1) the Jews who had the law given to them directly by God in written form, and (2) the Gentiles who, although they did not have the written law, nevertheless had a God-implanted instinctive knowledge of right and wrong within their hearts. Both would be judged by God, says Paul. The Jew on the basis of the written law; the Gentile on the basis of the law that was written not on tablets or books but in the heart, i. e., the conscience.

A Still Small Voice

Recall the story of the prophet Elijah. He was sitting under a juniper tree one day so depressed that he wanted to die. As we read of this incident in his life we suddenly come to the dramatic words, "And behold, the Lord passed by." How did the Lord pass by? " . . . and a great and strong wind rent the mountains and broke in pieces the rocks . . . but the Lord was not in the wind; and after the wind an earthquake; but the Lord was not in the earthquake; and after the earthquake a fire; but the Lord was not in the fire; and after the fire (after all the noise and the tumult) *a still small voice*"—inside Elijah. The "still small voice" of a sensitized conscience—that is how the Lord spoke to Elijah; that is how He speaks to us.

The Divine Umpire

In PARADISE LOST Milton pictures God saying as He is creating man, "I will put mine umpire, conscience, in his breast." What better definition of conscience can there be? The God-implanted umpire who calls the plays—fair or foul.

A Moral God

Somewhere in this universe there is a God—a Moral God—who wants us to do good and to avoid evil. He has given us many hints that He exists. One such hint is the voice of conscience which He planted in each one of us. This inner voice makes no sense unless there is a moral God standing behind it: Someone who is intensely interested that we do what is right. As John Baillie said, "It . . . is not simply your own voice. It is not just the beating of your own heart you are hearing. It is the beating of the heart of the universe." Nay, it is the beating of the heart of God; it is the cock that crows when we betray God.

The cock always crows when we deny life—as it crowed when Peter denied Jesus. We are always warned by that inner voice—conscience.

A Stop Light for Living

One day as a little girl and her father were driving down a rather busy street, a traffic light at the corner suddenly turned red. The father quickly applied his brakes.

"It is a good thing you stopped," said the little daughter, "because there is a policeman standing over there."

The father explained to her that he obeyed the signs whether there was a policeman on the corner or not.

After she thought for a while the little girl said, "You know, daddy, it would be a good idea if there were stop-lights for everything we did. Wouldn't it be wonderful if it would always turn red when there was danger ahead, and when everything was alright it would turn green?"

The father then went on to tell her that there really is a stop light for everyday living. He told her about the voice of conscience which says, "No" to try to stop us from doing wrong, and "Yes" to help us do that which is right.

Why Conscience Hurts

When a person sins, conscience reacts like a broken bone. As a broken bone hurts because it is not where it ought to be, so conscience hurts and pains us when it is not where it ought to be—in a right relationship to God. The deed we did, the word we said, the harm we wrought, the good we might have done—all these are brought back by conscience to trouble us. But why? For what reason? Is it because God is sadistic? Does He wish to inflict misery upon us? Does He want to twist life into something that hurts and cheapens? No! That's not the kind of God we believe in. God allows conscience to trouble us for one reason: to awaken us, to bring us to repentance, to guide us to a better way. A hurt conscience is God speaking to us, telling us that we have denied life; we have disobeyed Him. What pain is to the body (a warning that something is wrong, urging us to seek medical help), that is what a hurt conscience is to the soul.

Dr. Paul Tournier distinguishes between what he calls the *positive* conscience and the *negative* conscience. The negative conscience, he says, is the voice which says, "You have sinned." It accuses us. The positive conscience is the voice which says, "Confess it and receive God's forgiveness. God will not forsake you. Come to Him." "One is negative, the other positive; one crushes, the other is a call to deliverance and life." The purpose of conscience is to lead us from the negative to the positive. It is God calling us to new life.

The Need for Guidance

"Do not dishonor your conscience," says St. Maximus the Confessor, "which always gives you excellent counsel. For it offers you divine and angelic advice."

And St. John Climacus says, "After God, let us have conscience as our aim and rule in everything." But conscience itself is not a safe guide. It cannot stand by itself. It needs to be developed and sensitized by Godly training. Conscience is a safe guide only when it is properly educated and safely guided by the Holy Spirit. For conscience does not tell us what is right and what is wrong. It praises us for doing good without telling us what good is; it chastizes for doing evil without telling us what evil is. Conscience needs to be educated as to what is good and what is evil. We get out of it only what we put into it.

A man living out in the wilderness called a radio station once and asked them to sound the note A at an appointed time over the radio. "I have an old fiddle," he said, "and I'd like to tune it." This man realized that there was a standard and he called the radio station for it. God is our radio station. He gives us our standards. The fiddle is our conscience which must be constantly in tune with God and set according to His standard, His will. This we do every Sunday morning in church and every day in our prayers and personal devotions. We tune our conscience in to Christ and ask Him to give us the correct standard of right and wrong. Unless we tune our conscience in to God often, unless it is made captive to Christ and the Word of God, it will begin to give us wrong signals. It will become a false conscience.

"A good conscience," says St. Mark the Ascetic, "is found through prayer"—through the constant tuning of the mind and heart to God.

Conscience Has a Memory

Conscience has a memory—a terrible memory. It

haunts. Nobody else may know but I know and God knows and that is enough. The evil men do lives not *after* them, as Shakespeare said, but *with* them. Many records are kept of us in life, but the record we keep ourselves in our conscience is the most important one—the one we must live with, eat with, sleep with and die with. As Henry Thoreau said, "Public opinion is a weak tyrant compared with our private opinion."

Who judged Judas? Who condemned him? Who hanged him? Who put the cord around his neck? The disciples? The priests? The Romans? No! It was his conscience. He just couldn't bear to live with himself.

"A Continual Christmas"

This same inner voice that can cast us into a prison of remorse and guilt, and make life a veritable hell can also be the source of the greatest joy on earth. As one of the Church Fathers says, "To have an unaccusing conscience is indeed the pleasure of pleasures and the joy of joys." Nothing is a better tranquilizer than a clear conscience. There is no better applause than that which comes from one's own conscience. "A good conscience," said Benjamin Franklin, "is a continual Christmas." Years ago Augustine wrote: "A good conscience is the palace of Christ; the temple of the Holy Ghost; the paradise of delight; the standing Sabbath of the saints."

The poet George Herbert was on his way one day to hear an orchestra. On the road he saw a man struggling to get his cart out of the mud in the ditch. He stopped to help. It took such a long time that when he finally arrived he was told that the musical performance had ended. Someone said to him, "You have missed some of the finest music." George Herbert smiled and said, "Yes, but I shall be hearing songs at midnight." He would have the satisfaction of listening to the music of a happy conscience.

A little boy said once, "Inside of me I have a good feeling. It always comes when I have been kind to anyone; and I've found out what it is. It's God's thank you."

The Blood of Christ Purifies

St. Paul wrote, "Herein I also exercise myself *to have a conscience void of offense toward God and man.*" But who can have such a pure conscience "void of offense toward God and man"? We know what conscience can do. It can guide. It can warn. It can instruct. It can haunt. It can bless. But there is one thing conscience cannot do. It cannot undo the wrong we have done. It cannot heal the wounds it inflicts. It cannot eradicate guilt. It cannot forgive sin. Only Christ can do that. Only the blood of Christ can purify our conscience. Only He can forgive and heal and erase the past to bring to conscience "the peace of God which passes all understanding," to make us experience in conscience the joys of heaven.

PRAYER

Did I ever thank You, God, for my conscience, or thank You for this beautiful way of speaking to me. Forgive me, God, when I do not listen. Amen.

"HAVE NO ANXIETY ABOUT ANYTHING"

Palm Sunday (Philippians 4:4-9)

"Have no anxiety about anything, but in everything by prayer and supplication with thanksgiving let your requests be made known to God. And the peace of God which passes all understanding will keep your hearts and your minds in Christ Jesus" (Phil. 4:7-8).

"Have no anxiety about anything." When we hear these words, we feel like saying to St. Paul, "Come down to earth! Who can live like that? How can the business man, worried almost to the breaking point about inflation, not be anxious? How can the person afflicted with a malignancy not be anxious? How can a mother with a sick child not be anxious?

"Have no anxiety about anything." Now really, what kind of advice is that? Certainly, St. Paul must have been thinking of some other world and some other life! But he was not! When he wrote this advice he was having a pretty rough time of it. In fact, the words we heard in today's Epistle lesson were probably written from a prison cell not from an easy chair in front of a comfortable fireplace. St. Paul was no armchair philosopher. He was a realist, well acquainted with life.

"Have no anxiety about anything."

Bring It to God in Prayer

But Paul does not stop with these words. He goes on to give us the secret of how to overcome anxiety: " . . . but in everything by prayer and supplication with thanksgiving let your requests be made known to God." *Bring it to God*, he says. *Always, in everything!* You can talk to God about absolutely anything—anything whatever that is burdening your secret soul in the absolute knowledge and trust that He cares.

In the Old Testament Hezekiah received a disturbing letter from his enemy. It was the kind of letter that would cause a person sleepless nights. But Hezekiah having read the letter, "went up into the house of the Lord, and spread it before the Lord." Whatever the invading anxiety is, we can always "spread it out" before the Lord in prayer.

"Let not your heart be troubled," says Jesus. And He goes on to give us the secret of a trouble-free heart. "*Believe* in God, *believe* also in me." Trust Him completely. Spread it all out before Him in prayer.

Dietrich Bonhoeffer, the German theologian, was in prison at the time of the Second World War in Hitler's Germany. He was separated from his loved ones until the time of his execution. He was no stranger to anxiety. But through Christ he learned to overcome it. He wrote, "From the moment we wake until we fall asleep we must commend our loved ones wholly and unreservedly to God and leave them in His hands, transforming our anxiety for them into prayers on their behalf."

"In *nothing* be anxious but in *everything* by prayer and supplication with thanksgiving make your requests known unto God." This, then, is Paul's prescription for anxiety. Take it to the Lord in prayer. "Tell God every detail of your needs in earnest and thankful prayer" (J. B. Phillips). When Paul says, "Have no anxiety about anything," he does not mean that we are to be careless and indifferent about life. There are some things about which we ought to be concerned and anxious *but*, after we have done all we can do for them, we are to cast these burdens—every detail of them—upon the Lord, for He cares for us, as St. Peter says.

The English word *anxiety* is derived from the Latin word meaning *to choke.* A thing is choked when the outlet is blocked. That is exactly what causes over-anxiety. There is no outlet for our worries and fears. They back up on us, set nerves twitching, and fill our days and nights with fears. But we Christians have an outlet. We can let that pent-up flood of cares and anxieties flow into the ocean of God's compassion.

"In Everything"

"In everything . . . let your requests be made known to God." We lay special emphasis on this word "everything." Nothing is too small for God to handle. Nothing is too insignificant for His interest. We must never think that we insult God by making our trifling requests known to Him. Anything at all that may cause anxiety and worry is a reason for prayer. The Bible has purposely kept the area of request wide open. "In *everything* . . . let your requests be made known to God."

The outlet for our anxieties, then, is to "let our requests be made known to God," daily. "Come unto Me all you who labor and are heavy laden and I will give you rest," says Jesus. If we have no rest today, it is because we do not bring our anxieties to Jesus. We try to carry them alone. And they literally choke us.

Relinquishment

Jesus was no stranger to anxiety. He was terribly anxious in the Garden of Gethsemane just before His crucifixion. We hear Him saying, "Now my soul is troubled . . . Father, save me from this hour. . . . Remove this cup from me." But then comes prayer and relinquishment: " . . . nevertheless not my will be done but thine." After relinquishment comes peace: "Father, forgive them for they know not what they do . . . Father, into your hands I commend my spirit."

Thomas Merton said once, "Anxiety is inevitable in an age of crisis like ours. Don't make it worse by deceiving yourself and acting as if you were immune to all inner trepidation. God does not ask you not to feel anxious, but to trust in Him no matter how you feel."

"With Thanksgiving"

"In *nothing* be anxious, but in *everything* by prayer and supplication with *thanksgiving* let your requests be made known to God." Why does St. Paul bother to add "with thanksgiving"?

A lady visited a pastor one day. She had many troubles to pour out to him. He told her he would gladly listen *provided* she would first tell him all she had to be thankful for. She accepted his condition and for a solid half hour gave her many reasons for being thankful. After she had concluded, her pastor said, "Now you can tell me your troubles." To her surprise the lady found herself saying, "I really don't think I have any."

"Tell God every detail of your needs in earnest and thankful prayer." That is, check your blessings as well as your handicaps. Thank Him for all your blessings; list them one by one, name them, go over them, and, when you have finished, you may be surprised to find that the list of assets may be longer than the debits.

Fix Your Mind on Christ

The final cure for anxiety in today's Epistle lesson is expressed by St. Paul when he says, "Finally, brethren, whatever is true, whatever is honorable, whatever is just, whatever is pure, whatever is lovely, whatever is gracious, if there is any excellence, if there is anything worthy of praise, think about these things." I like J. B. Phillips' translation of this verse. Instead of "think about these things," he says, "*fix your minds*" on these things. In other words, in the midst of the storm of anxiety, fix your mind on Christ. Fix your mind on His power, on His love, on His great promises. Soak your mind with Christ and you will discover for yourself the truth of what Isaiah said, "Thou wilt keep him in perfect peace, *whose mind is stayed on Thee*; because he trusteth in Thee" (Is. 26:3).

Conclusion

"Have no anxiety about anything." These words may seem strange but only when they are taken out of context. They were never intended to stand alone. They are anchored on:

1. "In everything by prayer and supplication with thanksgiving let your requests be made known unto God."

2. Fix your mind on Christ, His power, His love, His promises. The result of this is not anxiety but peace, "the peace of God which passes all understanding" and keeps our minds and hearts in Jesus Christ.

PRAYER

Lord, who is not anxious? Who is not fearful? Who is not troubled in spirit as You were before Your crucifixion. We thank You that through prayer and relinquishment we can lay it all out before You and let You replace our anxiety with Your peace. Help us to fix our minds on You in every storm. Amen.

If Christ Has Not Been Raised

Easter Sunday (I Cor. 15:17-22)

> *"If Christ has not been raised, your faith is futile and you are still in your sins. Then those who have fallen asleep in Christ have perished. If for this life only we have hoped in Christ, we are of all men most to be pitied" (I Cor. 15:17-19).*

An atheist said once, "We don't need God anymore. Through science, technology, and education we not only know what our problems are, but we also know how to solve them." Someone asked him, "How do you solve the problem of death?" The atheist had no answer.

At Easter we celebrate the solution of the greatest problem man faces: death.

If there is no resurrection, says St. Paul, our faith is empty.

If there is no resurrection, we are still in our sins.

If there is no resurrection, our loved ones who have fallen asleep have perished.

If there is no resurrection, we have no hope; we are of all men most to be pitied.

If there is no resurrection, love stops with death. God's love cannot reach beyond the grave.

If there is no resurrection, there is no justice. The books will never be balanced. Truth, virtue, goodness will remain crucified forever.

"If Christ has not been raised, your faith is futile and you are still in your sins. Then those also who have fallen asleep in Christ have perished. If in this life we who are in Christ have only hope, we are of all men most to be pitied."

"But *in fact* Christ *has been* raised from the dead, the first fruits of those who have fallen asleep," continues St. Paul. "For as by a man came death, by a man has come also the resurrection of the dead. For as in Adam all die, so also in Christ shall all be made alive" (I Cor. 15:20-22). Because Christ did in fact rise from the dead, our faith is not futile; our sins are forgiven; our loved ones who have fallen asleep in the Lord have *not* perished; we do have hope; God's love does reach beyond the grave; there is justice.

A New Mood for Living

Christ's resurrection has created an entirely new mood for living. It has transformed us from the kingdom of darkness to the kingdom of light.

Death is still with us. But it is now a defeated enemy. Job's question: "If a man die, shall he live again?" is answered by the Resurrected Christ, "Whoever lives and believes in me has life eternal." The victory is Christ's!

It was this faith that enabled a person with a terminal illness to pray, "Dear Jesus, if You take me now, it is all right because wherever I go I will be with You."

Suffering is still with us. But it is now a defeated enemy. "I reckon that the sufferings of the present moment are not worthy to be compared with the glory that will be revealed to us in the life to come," says Paul. "In the world you have tribulation, but be of good cheer, I have overcome the world," said Jesus. The victory is Christ's!

Sin is still with us. But now as a defeated enemy. Through Christ we have forgiveness; we have also the power to overcome. "We are more than conquerors through Him who loved us." No matter what kind of tomb you have buried yourself in through sin, Christ can liberate you. The victory is Christ's!

Evil is still with us. But now as a defeated enemy. On Good Friday we may have said of Christ, "If this is what happens to a good man, why should one lead a good life?" But on Easter Sunday we know that that is not what happens to a good man. Virtue will always triumph. Ultimately evil will be overcome. This is what the second coming of Jesus is all about. The victory is Christ's!

A German pastor was accused of high treason by the Nazis and sentenced to death. Before the execution the godless hangman wanted to make his last joke with the man of God. Flaunting his pistol, the hangman sneered, "Five minutes yet, then it is all over. Where is your Almighty God now?"

Trembling in voice but steady in heart the pastor replied, "Oh, yes; that you have the power today, any child can see. Maybe you will have it tomorrow, too. But don't forget, there will still be a third day. And that belongs to God." With these words he died.

The "third day" always belongs to God and to those who are living members of His Body—the Church. The victory is Christ's!

Our Easter liturgy concludes with the beautiful words of St. John Chrysostom:

"O Death, where is thy sting? O Hades, where is thy victory? Christ is risen and thou art overthrown. Christ is risen and the demons have fallen. Christ is risen and the Angels rejoice. Christ is risen and life is liberated. Christ is risen and there is none dead in the tomb. For Christ is raised from the dead, and become the first-fruits of them that slept. To Him be glory and power from all Ages to all Ages."

Peter's Healing Shadow

Sunday of St. Thomas (Acts 5:12-20)

"Now many signs and wonders were done among the people by the hands of the apostles . . . And more than ever believers were added to the Lord, multitudes both of men and women, so that they even carried out the sick into the streets, and laid them on beds and pallets, that as Peter came by at least his shadow might fall on some of them" (Acts 5:12, 14-15).

The early apostles were so filled with the power of the Holy Spirit that wherever they went they accomplished "signs and wonders." In fact, the Apostle Peter's influence was so great that sick people were carried out and placed on the street so that Peter's shadow might fall on them to heal them.

Your Shadow

Everyone has a shadow. Everyone exerts an influence on others either for good or bad. The impact of our personality on another makes it either easier or harder for the person to live the good life. No one is neutral. No one counts for nothing. We cannot escape from this any more than we can escape casting a shadow on a sunny day, and it is either a shadow of healing or a shadow of harm.

The Greeks have a phrase "ehi kalo iskio" or "Kaloiskiotos" to describe a person who has a good shadow and is thus blessed. Even now in India, a Brahmin will throw away his rice if the shadow of an outcaste falls across it. Indian people used to try to get themselves in a position so that Ghandi's shadow might fall upon them and bring them blessing. So one is not surprised to read in the Book of Acts that they carried the sick into the streets, "that, as Peter passed by at least his shadow might fall on some of them" (Acts 5:15).

Nutritious Vs. Toxic Persons

A director of nursing said once, "When I train nurses I say to them, 'Be a nutritious person; don't be a toxic person.' "

She went on to say, "We have some nurses in our hospitals who are toxic people. Whenever they come into a room and either talk with a patient or touch them, they infect that person with the poison of fear, doubt and anxiety. Everything they do and say tears people down.

"We also have nurses who are nutritious persons," she continued. "The way they talk, the way they touch, the way they listen, the way they offer encouragement and the way they build hope, always puts nutritional strength into the patient. They create a mental attitude in which God can perform a healing ministry."

Healing Shadows

A true Christian, like Peter, is a nutritious person.

He casts a healing shadow. Phillips Brooks, the great preacher, walked down a Boston street one gloomy day and greeted a merchant, who thereupon said, "It was a cloudy day until Phillips Brooks came by and then it was as if the sun broke through the clouds." He had a healing shadow.

One morning in 1888, Nobel, the inventor of dynamite, awoke to read in the newspaper his own obituary. Of course, it was a mistake. His brother had died and the newspaper carelessly reported the death of the wrong brother. Any man would be disturbed under the circumstances, but to Alfred Nobel the shock was overwhelming. He saw himself as the world saw him—"the dynamite king," the great industrialist who had made an immense fortune from explosives. This—as far as the general public was concerned—was the entire purpose of his life. None of his true intentions—to break down the barriers that separated men and ideas—were recognized or given serious consideration. He was quite simply a merchant of death, and for that alone would he be remembered. This was the dark shadow he would leave behind him. As he read his obituary he was so horror stricken that he resolved to make clear to the world the true meaning and purpose of his life. This could be done through the final disposition of his fortune. His last will and testament would be the expression of his life's ideals. The result was that he established the most valued of prizes to be given to those who have done most for the cause of world peace—the Nobel Prize. He left a shadow that even today motivates people to work for world peace.

Let me share with you one final example. Into a church one Sunday morning there walked a disheveled young man who had walked the streets all night. He didn't much care what people thought of his looks, for he was deeply disturbed. He had lost his grip on the meaning and purpose of life. He had lost his contact with God. He was so miserable that he had begun to wonder whether life was worthwhile. He decided to sit in the back pew of the church and listen once more to a sermon. He sat numb through the entire service. Suddenly he noticed his science professor across the aisle.

The professor had bent forward, head bowed in an attitude of humble prayer. The student watched him, and when the prayer was over, he noticed that the professor's face was quiet and restful. Peace and contentment were written all over it. The student was so deeply impressed that he said to himself as he slipped out quietly after the service, "My goodness, if my professor believes in God and prayer and has peace written all over him, maybe it's not such a crazy idea after all."

The end result was that this young man went on to become a great medical missionary. The professor never realized what a tremendous effect the shadow of his example had on this young man.

The Secret of a Healing Shadow

We all cast a shadow in life. We affect the people we live with every time we are with them. We wind up making others either more hopeful about themselves, or less hopeful. Simon Peter cast a shadow that healed. The person who stands with the light of Christ upon him will cast a shadow that has healing in it. The person who lives in Christ, as Peter did; who enters God's presence through prayer every day and is filled with the Holy Spirit cannot but be a nutritious person whose shadow radiates to others the love, hope, peace, joy, and strength of Christ.

The Church Fathers used to say, "The one who goes into the perfume shop every day, even if he buys nothing, leaves the shop with a fragrance about him." The perfume shop is God's presence which we may enter daily through prayer. ". . . through us (God) spreads the fragrance of the knowledge of Him everywhere. For we are the aroma of Christ. . ." (II Cor. 2:14-15).

PRAYER

Lord, when my shadow falls
behind me, let whatever it
falls on be blessed. Let it
not turn others off, but let it
turn them on to You. Amen.

Preaching the Word and Serving at Tables

Sunday of the Myrrh-bearing Women (Acts 6:1-7)

"It is not right that we should give up preaching the Word of God to serve tables. Therefore, brethren, pick out from among you seven men of good repute, full of the Spirit and of wisdom, whom we may appoint to this duty" (Acts 6:2-3).

Today's Epistle lesson shows us how the early apostles felt about preaching the word and serving the needy poor. They considered both tasks important—different aspects of the same ministry. They would continue their ministry of preaching the word. For the other ministry of serving the needy widows they ordained seven "men of good repute, full of the Spirit and of wisdom"—the first deacons.

The Deacon

The word deacon, derived from the Greek "diakonos," means to serve others. It has in it the very essence of Christianity: serving and caring for others in humble love. It has been said that the clergy, who are ordained first as deacons (servants) must remain deacons throughout life whether they go on later to become priests, bishops or even patriarchs. A true Christian is always first and foremost a deacon, a servant. The charter of service for deacons, or servants, was given by Jesus when He said, "You know that those who are supposed to rule over the Gentiles lord it over them, and their great men exercise authority over them. But it shall not be so among you; but whoever would be great among you must be your servant, and whoever will be first among you must be slave of all. For the Son of Man also came not to be served but to serve, and to give his life a ransom for many" (Mark 10:42-45).

Jesus: A Deacon

He who is Lord of the universe chose to come to us in the form of a diakonos, a deacon or servant: "Have this mind among yourselves, which you have in Christ Jesus, who, though he was in the form of God, did not count equality with God a thing to be grasped, but emptied himself, taking the form of a servant . . ." (Phil. 2:5-7).

One of the supreme examples of Jesus as diakonos, deacon or servant, is found in the Gospel of John: "Jesus, knowing that the Father had given all things into his hands, and that he had come from God and was going to God, rose from supper, laid aside his garments, and girded himself with a towel. Then he poured water into a basin, and began to wash the disciples' feet, and to wipe them with the towel with which he was girded . . . When he had washed their feet . . . he said to them, 'Do you know what I have done for you? You call me Teacher and Lord; and you are right, for so I am. If I then, your Lord and Teacher, have washed your feet, you also ought to wash one another's feet. For I have given you an example, that you also should do as I have done" (John 13:3-5, 12-15).

Jesus was a deacon not only in that He washed the disciples' feet but also in that He offered the supreme sacrifice for us on the cross.

Two Bowls of Water

In the Gospels we read about two bowls of water. One is the bowl of water in which Pilate washed his hands when he was shelving his responsibility for the fate of Jesus. Pilate symbolically washed his hands of responsibility. The other is the bowl of water Jesus used to wash His disciples' feet, to demonstrate the need for His followers to be humble and willing to serve one another.

Which bowl of water are we using? The one in which we wash our hands of responsibility? Or the one where we accept responsibility and go out in loving service to others? We come to church to sit but do we go out to serve suffering humanity in the name of Christ?

The Greatest Disease Today

Mother Teresa of India said once:

"The biggest disease today is not leprosy or tuberculosis, but rather the feeling of being unwanted, uncared for, and deserted by everybody. The greatest evil is lack of love, the terrible indifference towards one's neighbors who live at the roadside assaulted by exploitation, poverty and diseases.

"The unwanted are hungry not for food but for love; they are thirsty not for water but for peace; they are naked not for clothes but for dignity; they are homeless not for shelter but for understanding.

"You may feel your efforts do not count. We ourselves feel that what we are doing is just a drop in the ocean. But if that drop was not in the ocean, I think the ocean would be less because of that missing drop. Even your feeble efforts will bear much fruit if you bring God in your life . . ."

Most of us never have a chance to do big things for someone but all of us have the opportunity to do a million little things for people in need. For example:

I can speak a word of encouragement to one of God's children.

I can write a letter—not out of necessity, but simply to let someone know that I am thinking of him.

I can radiate a blessing to someone. (A blessing is a wish for happiness directed toward any person.)

I can be a listening post for someone in need of unburdening himself.

I can say things to another person and do things for other persons—kind and considerate things.

If a helping hand is needed, I can lend my hand.

If there is anyone I can help without his knowing I helped, I gladly serve in this way.

I can be courteous—even to those who are curt and unfriendly.

There are so many ways that I can be a blessing to someone!

Always the greatest service, the greatest help I can give to someone is my sincere prayer.

A story is told of Albert Schweitzer, the great philosopher, musician and theologian. When he was a student in Strasbourg, he met an old woman on the street. He learned in his talk with her that she had no mattress. He went straight home, took the mattress off his own bed, and carried it on his back through the streets to where the elderly woman lived. He was a true servant, deacon, following in the footsteps of his Master.

How Is God Best Revealed Today?

Some time ago a television interviewer questioned representatives of all the major religions of the world concerning the ways in which they sought God and how they thought He could best be revealed to men. The Muslim took him to a mosque at the time of praying as the masses bowed in that attitude of "submission" which is the literal meaning of the word "Islam." The Hindu showed him the ritual of sacrifice within the temple. The Jew read to him in a synagogue the sacred writings of the prophets. Then came the turn of the Christian, an Indian. He took the TV interviewer not to a Church, not even to the Bible, but into a home for lepers. As the camera ranged over the deformed and disfigured patients who had once been discarded by society but who were now gathered into a loving and caring community, he said that it was in those faces that he saw the beauty of Jesus, transfiguring them, changing them from glory into glory, not only as they received healing but even more as they knew themselves loved and accepted for Jesus' sake.

Here then is how God is best revealed to the world today: through humble service in the name of Jesus.

The Supremacy of Service

In the tradition of the Orthodox Church when the monks are forced to make a distinction between prayer life and active Christian life, very often they give priority to the active life of service. When someone asked a certain old monk saying, "There be two brothers, and one of them is quiet in his cell, and prolongs his fast for six days, and lays much travail on himself, but the other cares for the sick. Whose work is the more acceptable to God?" The old monk answered, "If that brother who carries his fast for six days were to hang himself by the nostrils, he could not equal the other, who does service to the sick."

A Serving Community

At a small chapel on the famed Duomo Square in Florence, Italy, there is an inconspicuous door on which the words appear MISERICORDIA FRATERNITY. The Misericordia Brotherhood was founded in Florence in 1246, by a group of Florentine aristocrats who discovered during a terrible plague (which wiped out a third of the population) that to be a Christian is to be a servant of others, a deacon. Donning black robes and masks to make them anonymous, these aristocrats worked as stretcher bearers among the helpless and poor.

The brotherhood still continues its serving, providing most of the ambulance service and much of the welfare work in Tuscany. Today, men of all classes belong to the Misericordia Brotherhood, from laborers to nobility, each serving at least one hour a week, shaving a bedfast old man, bathing an invalid, or performing other personal service. The ancient tradition of anonymity continues, however, so that the emphasis is on serving, without thought of personal acclaim. For over 700 years, the Misericordia Brotherhood has observed the practice of thanking those they have helped, crossing their arms, bowing, and saying to those they have just served, "Thank you for needing me!"

These Christians are true deacons serving Jesus in the world today!

To keep us ever humble as servants we need to remember that serving God is *not* what we do *for* God; it is what we let *God* do *through* us!

A mother whose child was healed at Dr. Schweitzer's hospital in Africa reached down and kissed the back of his hand. As she did, she left two tiny tears there.

Holding the two tears up to his friends, Dr. Schweitzer said, "These two diamonds of love are the only reward that I seek for my labors."

No greater reward can come to us, as Christians, than the inner satisfaction of knowing that God has been pleased to use us as channels through which to bless others.

"Inasmuch as you have done it unto one of these the least of my brethren," said Jesus, "you have done it to me."

Truly there is no calling higher or more noble than that of a deacon, a servant.

PRAYER

Lord, make me an instrument of Your peace.
Where there is hatred, let me sow love;
Where there is injury, pardon;
Where there is doubt, faith;
Where there is despair, hope;
Where there is darkness, light;
Where there is sadness, joy.
O Divine Master, grant that I may not so much seek to be consoled as to console;
To be understood as to understand;

To be loved as to love;
For it is in giving that we receive;
It is in pardoning that we are pardoned;
It is in dying that we are born to eternal life.

—St. Francis of Assisi

Power To Rise Above Life's Woes

Sunday of the Paralytic (Acts 9:32-42)

The Epistle lesson today tells of a man named Aeneas who had been bedridden for eight years as a paralytic. Upon seeing him the apostle Peter said, "Aeneas, Jesus Christ heals you; rise and make your bed." Immediately he rose.

The second miracle in the Epistle lesson concerns a disciple named Tabitha, a woman who "was full of good works and acts of charity." She became ill. Peter was summoned to heal her. By the time he arrived she was dead. Putting out the women who were weeping, Peter knelt down and prayed; then turning to the body he said, "Tabitha, rise." She opened her eyes and sat up. When this miracle became known, many believed in the Lord.

The Gospel lesson tells of a third miracle concerning an invalid who waited for healing at the pool at Bethesda. For 38 years he waited. To this poor, abandoned invalid Jesus said, "Rise, take your pallet and walk." At once the man was healed. He took up his pallet and walked.

It is interesting that in each one of these three miracles the word RISE is used:

"Aeneas, Jesus Christ heals you; *RISE* and make your bed."

"Tabitha, *RISE.*"

"*RISE,* take up your pallet and walk."

The word *RISE* is the key word in today's Epistle and Gospel readings. We shall concentrate our attention on this single, all-important word "RISE."

"Rise"

The whole message of the Gospel is contained in that little word "rise." Jesus raises us from the depths of sin and death to a new life of peace and power. When Peter begins to sink into the sea because of his little faith, Jesus reaches out to raise him, as He raised us in the waters of baptism lifting us from sin and death to newness of life.

He Raises Us From the Abyss

The icon of the Resurrection in the Orthodox Church is in reality the icon of His Descent into Hell. In the West, the Resurrection of our Lord is depicted as a victorious rising from the tomb. Jesus is depicted alone. In the East, the Resurrection is proclaimed by the image of the glorified Christ descending into the abyss. In the words of the troparion: "In the tomb with the body, in hell with the soul as God . . ." Even while the body of Jesus was in the tomb those three days, His love was active. He used that time to descend with His soul into the very depths of hell, into the abyss of death, there to break the bonds of death and to proclaim to those who lived before Him the good news of salvation. He, the

Second Adam, the perfect Man, reaches out to touch, renew and raise into His glory the First Adam, the man who had fallen from life, who dwelt in the land of the shadow.

This descent, this final and ultimate penetration into the realm of death, is accomplished by Christ. The Resurrection icon shows Christ—not standing alone—but raising, lifting Adam and Eve out of the depths through the broken doors of hell. He frees patriarch, prophet and king. But, at the same time He frees us. He sets at liberty our own life. The hand that reaches out to grasp the hand of Adam reaches out to embrace Adam's descendants as well. For we, too, are bound by death. We, too, are held captive by the power of sin. We, too, have "died" and been cast into the farthest reaches of the abyss. Yet the Risen Savior comes to us as to lost sheep, descending in His compassionate love to seek us out in the darkness and to raise us up with Himself. Like the Hound of Heaven, He pursues us down the byways. If we make our bed in hell, He is there, ever present, ever reaching out to raise us with Him into the glory of the resurrected life. From anxiety in the face of death, He raises us to an unshakeable hope in the resurrected life. From fear of the future, He raises us to undiminished joy. From loneliness and separation, He raises us to friendship with God. Because He is risen, He has the power to help us rise from the tombs of slavery, sin, and death to fullness of life.

"Aeneas, Jesus Christ heals you; *rise . . .*"

"Tabitha, *rise.*"

"*Rise,* take up your pallet and walk."

"Religion is Moonshine"

There are those who say cynically, "Religion is moonshine." I could not agree with them more fervently especially when I remember that it is the power of the moon that lifts trillions of tons of water each day to make the tides rise in the oceans of the world. In the moon there is power enough to stagger man's imagination. Greater than the moon's power is the power of Him Who created the moon—power to help us rise from the deepest abysses in life. "*Rise,* take up your pallet and walk."

He Raised Lazarus

A friend was asked, "Do you really believe Jesus raised Lazarus from the dead?" The reply was, "I never knew Lazarus, but I know what Jesus did for me. I understand Lazarus had been dead only four days. I had been dead four years.

"I had gone to pieces—I was both down and out. My family had gone to pieces; my wife and children had let me down. My business was gone. Everything was chaos.

"Then Jesus spoke to me, and I became alive again. Now my loved ones have come back. My friends recognize me. All things are made new. I do not know much about Lazarus, but one thing I do know—Jesus lifted me out of death into a new life." "Tabitha, *rise!*"

We all have troubles in life. What we need more than anything else is power to rise above them. But we cannot rise above our troubles and difficulties unless we have within us Him Who helps us rise, the Lord Jesus. He by Whose power Aeneas was raised; Tabitha was raised; the invalid by the pool of Bethesda was raised; this same Jesus gives us the power today to *RISE* above whatever obstacles life can place in our way.

PRAYER

Lord, when I look at the Resurrection icon, I know that in holding Adam's hand to raise him from the abyss, it is my hand You are holding to lift me from my sins and woes into Your very Presence. Thank You, Lord, for the uplifting power of Your love. Amen.

In Antioch the Disciples Were for the First Time Called Christians

Sunday of the Samaritan Woman (Acts 11:1930)

" . . . and in Antioch the disciples were for the first time called Christians" (Acts 11:26).

The name "Christian" was first given to the followers of Jesus in Antioch. Antioch was notorious for its ability to produce nicknames. They had one even for the emperor whom they once called "the Goat." Thus the name "Christian" was given to the followers of Jesus neither by themselves nor by the Jews, but by the Greek-speaking pagans in Antioch. It was a nickname, a by-word, given in derision and contempt.

The Christians took this name given in mockery and turned it into one of the most revered names in history. The name tells us something very important about the Christian: that there is a resemblance between Christ and the Christian. The Christian is first and foremost a CHRIST person.

A New Name For a New People

The people in Antioch had many names in their resourceful language but they had no name to cover this type of character. These followers of Jesus did things, said things, lived things hitherto unheard of in the history of the world. They lived purity—purity of a new order, purity of thought and feeling. They lived forgiveness—forgiveness of a new kind, forgiveness for friend and foe alike. They lived love—love of a new order, love for those who least deserved it. They lived humility—a new kind of humility the world had not seen before *except in Jesus!* So they made a new name for these people in whom they saw the purity, the forgiveness, the love, and the humility of Jesus. They called them CHRISTIANOI, Christ people! There was something so new about these people, something so refreshingly different, that they coined a new name for them. " . . . and in Antioch the disciples were for the first time called Christians" (Acts 11:26).

The Early Christians

In 248 A.D. Cyprian, the Bishop of Carthage, wrote the following to his friend Donatus about Christians:

"This seems to be a cheerful world, Donatus, when I view it from this fair garden under the shadow of these vines. But if I climb some great mountain and look out over the wide lands, you know very well what I would see—brigands on the road, pirates on the seas, in the amphitheaters men murdering each other to please the applauding crowds, and under all roofs I see misery and selfishness. It is really a bad world, Donatus, an incredibly bad world. Yet in the midst of it, I have found a quiet and holy people. They have discovered a joy which is a thousand times better than any pleasure of this sinful life. They are despised and persecuted but they care not. These people, Donatus, are Christians and I am one of them."

They were a different people, those early Christians, conformed not to the world but to Christ. Christ people!

The Athenian orator Aristides, writing to the Emperor Hadrian (117-138 A.D.), described the early Christians as follows:

"The Christians know and trust God . . . They do good to their enemies. They love one another . . . They rescue the orphan from him who does him violence . . . If anyone among them is poor and needy, and they do not have food to spare, they fast for two or three days, that they may supply him with necessary food. They scrupulously obey the commands of their Messiah. Every morning and every hour they thank and praise God for His loving-kindness toward them. . . . Because of them there flows forth all the beauty that there is in the world. But the good deeds they do, they do not proclaim in the ears of the multitude, but they take care that no one shall perceive them. . . Truly, *this is a new people* and *there is* something divine in them."

A new name had to be found for those new people—a name that expressed the Christ Who lived in them and made them "the salt of the earth and the light of the world.": CHRISTIANS! CHRIST PEOPLE! " . . . and in Antioch the disciples were for the first time called Christians" (Acts 11:26).

What's in a Name?

What's in a name? The first thing that should exist in a name is a resemblance of the one named to the one after whom one is named. Alexander the Great once found a soldier in his ranks who was accused of cowardice in the face of the enemy. When asked his name, the soldier replied, "Alexander." Whereupon Alexander the Great replied, "Either change your name or change your behavior." Some of us, who bear the name "Christian" lightly, need to heed Alexander's advice.

What Is a Christian

Sometimes people ask, "What is a Christian? How do I know if I am a Christian?" If someone were to ask you, "Why are you a Christian?" what would you reply? Would you say, "I am a Christian because. . . ." Because of what? Because you were born in a Christian family? Because you were baptized? Because you try to do good? Because you try to practice the golden rule? To be a Christian means far more than that.

To see exactly what it means let us go back to the very first Christians, the twelve apostles. How did they become Christians? One day Jesus said to them, "Follow me!" "And they forsook their nets and followed Him."

Here we have our answer. A Christian is someone who follows Christ consciously and by personal choice, who responds to His call, who says "Yes" to Him. First and always it is a relationship to a Person—not to a code or philosophy.

To be a Christian is to be committed to God in Christ. It is to be a living member of His Body, the Church. It is to be under compulsion to live a certain kind of life—the life of Christ.

When a famous person was asked why he was a Christian, he replied, "The world is full of fantasy; there must be some reality somewhere, and the only reality that I've found is the reality of the Christian faith." To be a Christian is to have found reality in Christ.

If I can say, "My name is Christian," it is a truth far greater in value than any human being can possibly conceive. To be a son or daughter of God, loved by God the Father, redeemed by God the Son, indwelt by God the Holy Spirit, guaranteed His eternal and abundant riches—all this is beyond one's wildest dreams. Yet all this is mine, for my name is Christian!

The privilege of being a Christian bears a responsibility—the responsibility of knowing that I am here not to blow my own horn but to glorify Christ, to be His servant in today's world, to work for Him, and speak for Him, and bear a cross for Him, to deny self, to minister to the sick, the weak, the hungry, the oppressed in His Name.

"Have I Ever Seen a Christian?"

A little boy once asked his father, "What is a Christian?" The father, who knew the Bible well, described to his son what being a Christian really is according to the New Testament. So thoroughly did he explain the matter that when he was through, the little fellow said, "Father, have I ever seen a Christian?"

The early pagans in Antioch saw Christians. In fact, they saw Christ in His followers—so much so that they called them by the very name of Christ. Does the world today see something of Christ's love, His forgiveness, His humility in us? Is or life-style, our words and deeds, a witness of our faith in Christ?

When asked for the definition of a Christian, a person pointed to a friend he knew and said, "There goes a Christian!" He was a person whose life could not be explained apart from Christ.

Can anyone point to you or me and say the same? Why not? If my faith is real, if my commitment is true, if Jesus comes first in my life, if He is my ALL, if "for me to live is Christ," why not? Why shouldn't Christ show in my everyday life as He did in the lives of the early Christians?

They Just Shine

Jesus said, "Let your light so shine before men that they may see your good works and give glory to your Father in heaven." Christians are people who shine for Christ. As William Sangster said once, "They don't try to shine: they just shine. It is an event to meet them. When they come into a room it is like the light being turned on. They seem to have some secret of inner happiness, of poise, of patience, and an inexhaustible capacity for love. They never speak ill of anyone else; they praise people who surpass them and do it with complete sincerity; they seldom talk of themselves and they listen when you are talking to them as though your thoughts were the most interesting thoughts they had ever heard. They are quietly strong. They leave an impression of utter goodness. Without knowing it, they put an ache in you to have this quality of life as well." *

It was because of such a Christ-like life-style that the early followers of Jesus came to be called Christians. " . . . and in Antioch the disciples were for the first time called Christians" (Acts 11:26).

Would anyone be able to look at me today and guess that I am a Christian?

PRAYER

Lord Jesus, I bear Your holy name. Send Your Holy Spirit to abide in me to help me bear also Your holy life: Your love, Your forgiveness, Your humility. Amen.

---

*"Holiness" (Pharos Paper) by William E. Sangster.

"What Must I Do to Be Saved?"

Sunday of the Healing of the One Born Blind (Acts 16:16-34)

Every day that we live we are faced with various questions we have to answer:

"What am I going to wear today?"

"What am I going to prepare for breakfast, dinner, lunch?"

"What am I going to do when I graduate from high school?"

"Whom shall I marry?"

"Where shall we build or buy a home?"

All of these questions have significance, and all of them have a certain relative importance to life and to its happiness.

But there is one question above every other question—the question which the jailer in today's Epistle lesson asked Paul and Silas, "Sirs, what must I do to be saved?"

Whenever we hear the word "saved" some people think immediately of hell or heaven. Being saved means to them just that: escaping hell, achieving heaven. This is true, but it's a very limited way to think of this word "saved." For instance, it puts the whole matter in the future. We tend to forget, as a result, that we can be saved here and now while we are on this earth.

Saved from what? you ask. Saved from the things that make life turn sour on us.

Saved from Boredom

We speak of the meaninglessness of life and the boredom of it all. The expression "Fed up at fifteen, fagged out at forty" pretty much describes our generation.

More sin is caused by boredom than by anything else. Men and women will do almost anything to escape it. They will drink, drug themselves, sell their bodies and their souls, fling themselves into crazy causes. Yet what is boredom but the empty heart crying out, seeking for the only One Who can fill it to complete satisfaction: the Lord Jesus Christ. "He who drinks of this water shall thirst again," said Jesus to the Samaritan woman, "but he who drinks of the water that I shall give him will never thirst." "Sirs, what must I do to be saved?" Jesus can save us now from the meaninglessness and the boredom of life.

Saved from the Crowd

We speak of our "crowd culture." A distinguished American sociologist has divided people into those who are *inner-directed* and those who are *other-directed.* The inner-directed are those whose important decisions in life are made from inner convictions and an inner voice; the other-directed are those who take their color and goal from the people around them.

The other-directed are those who say, "When in Rome, do as the Romans do." But they neglect to ask which Romans: the poor? the middle class? the rich? the clergy? the men who sell bananas? the pornographers? the Communists? the Pope? They are all in Rome. Often the other-directed person is not one person but twenty different persons in one, being pulled in twenty different directions. The inner-directed person, on the other hand, is in constant communication with the Heart and Mind of the Universe. He finds meaning and direction in God's purpose and will. Through prayer, the Sacraments, the Bible, the Liturgy, and the Church he is in tune with the Lord Jesus Christ Who guides him as constantly and as faithfully as the radio beam guides the plane in the skies. "Sirs, what must I do to be saved?" Jesus can save us now from the tyranny of the crowd and make us inner-directed, God-directed people.

Saved from the Despair of our Age

We speak of the anxiety and the despair which possess the people of our age. The Danish philosopher Kierkegaard once said, "What is anxiety? It is the next day." Much of our anxiety is caused by "the next day," by a fear of the future. We are haunted by the possibility of total annihilation in nuclear war. We are threatened by the constant uncertainties of life: illness, separation from loved ones and, above all, the fear of death—our death.

It is to this anxiety that the word of God addresses itself when it says through the Apostle Paul: "Have no anxiety about anything, but in everything by prayer and supplication with thanksgiving let your requests be made known to God. And the peace of God, which passes all understanding, will keep your hearts and minds in Christ Jesus" (Phil. 4:6-7). "Who shall separate us from the love of Christ? Shall tribulation, or distress, or persecution, or famine . . . or peril, or sword? . . . No, in all these things we are more than conquerors through Him Who loved us. For I am sure that neither death nor life . . . nor anything else in all creation, will be able to separate us from the love of God in Christ Jesus our Lord" (Romans 8:35-39). The end of man is not death. "Whoever lives and believes in Me," said Jesus, "has passed from death to life." The end of the world will not be nuclear annihilation but Christ Who will come again to establish His everlasting Kingdom. "Sirs, what must I do to be saved?" Jesus can save us now from the anxiety and the despair of our age.

Saved from the Moral Looseness of Our Age

We speak of the moral looseness of our age, especially our sexual immorality. A German author (Erik Von Kuehnelt-Leddihn) writes,

"Imagine a man, driven by sheer lust, who engaged in an adulterous affair. In order to achieve his end, he has to pretend to be in love with the woman in question and immediately a stream of lies develops. He lies to her and to his wife. She lies to her husband. He has to lie to others to protect himself and her. In order to keep her affection he showers her with gifts he cannot afford. He makes money dishonestly to cover his expenses. She may become pregnant, again an invitation to new sins, one greater than the other.

"If one draws up a list of all the sins and other calamities which . . . can be expected to develop from sins of the flesh, one would not know where to begin and end: lies and theft, forgery and pretense, hypocrisy and abortion, neglect of sacramental life and suicide, murder, jealousy, hatred, anger, despair, fatherless children, and mothers tormented by permanent lies about a child's father."

When sex is abused it turns against the one who abuses it to destroy him or her. "I took what I wanted until I hated what I took," said one who had been promiscuous. The forgiveness of the Savior can save us now from the guilt, the despair, the emptiness of sexual immorality. For sex is a gift of God—a gift which finds its supreme fulfillment when it is used in accordance with the purpose for which God created it: for the expression of love and the procreation of life within the marital relationship.

"Sirs, what must I do to be saved?" Jesus can save us now through repentance and the power of the Holy Spirit from the hell of immoral living.

False Saviors

Yet some people have been tempted to believe that man does not need Jesus as a Savior anymore. Science has progressed to the point where it can save us from almost everything, they say. Science—not Jesus—is the new Savior!

Man needs science. But science is not the savior. Man does not live by science alone. Science can modernize a house, but it can never turn a house into a home. Jesus can! Science can make penicillin for the healing of the body, but it cannot minister to a guilty conscience. Jesus can! Science can put terrifying power into the hands of man, but not necessarily the moral strength to use this power wisely. Jesus can! "Neither is there salvation in any other: for there is no other name under heaven given among men, whereby we must be saved."

"Believe in the Lord Jesus"

"Sirs, what must I do to be saved?" And they said, "Believe in the Lord Jesus, and you will be saved." This, then, is the key to salvation: "*Believe* in the Lord Jesus."

What Does It mean to Believe in Jesus?

It means to rest the whole weight of your life on Jesus.

It means to bet your whole life on Him.

Ernest T. Campbell said once, "The man who makes his way to the two-dollar window of the race track to place a bet on a horse is wrong. He is wrong, not because he is gambling—but because he is not gambling enough! He is guilty of perverting an instinct. Putting two dollars on a horse is a shameful substitute for putting one's whole life on God." To believe in Jesus is to bet your whole life on Him.

When we were baptized our godparent confessed belief in Christ for us because we were not yet of age. He said the "I believe . . ." of the Nicene Creed for us. But if we are to be true Christians, there must come a time in life when we must say these words for ourselves—a time when we ourselves decide to follow Christ as our personal Lord and Savior and commit our whole life to Him as our God. Unless this happens we are not Orthodox Christians. We are Christians in name only; Christians by baptismal certificate only—to whom the Gospel of Christ means little or nothing.

"Sirs, what must I do to be saved?" And they said,

"Believe in the Lord Jesus, and you will be saved. . . ."

A baptismal certificate alone is not enough. Payment of church dues alone is not enough. Occasional church attendance alone is not enough. "Believe, lean your whole weight, bet your whole life upon the Lord Jesus, and you will be saved. . . ."

It took an earthquake to make the jailer ask Paul and Silas the question: "Sirs, what must I do to be saved?" Will it take another earthquake to make us ask the same question? Haven't we had enough earthquakes? All the wars, the anxiety, the despair, the meaninglessness, the boredom, the immorality of our age? Do we need something more devastating than these to make us ask the question, "What must I do to be saved?"

What Is Salvation?

"Believe in the Lord Jesus and you will be *saved*."

What does it mean to be "saved"? A newly "born-again" Christian went to a ball game. He was anxious to ask someone, "Are you saved?" Suddenly a person asked him: "Is the seat next to you saved?" He shot back, "No! Are you?" What does it mean to be saved? It means:

forgiveness of sins,
coming from darkness to light,
the destruction of death,
healing,
liberation from the slavery of Satan and his destructive power,
participating and sharing in the new life of Christ,
restoration of communion with God and fellowship with Him,
the transfiguration of man.

Salvation is not saying like the Pharisee, "Lord, see how good I am, how I fast, how I pray, how I give to the church. Would that others were as 'saved' as I am." Salvation is hiding one's eyes from God like the publican and saying humbly, "Lord, be merciful to me a sinner and save me."

Salvation is not a state of being but a motion, a journey that begins at baptism, a pilgrimage toward theosis, toward God, toward our promised land. There are those who are good starters but poor finishers. They begin the journey well at baptism but never finish it.

Salvation is not what I am, but what I am becoming in Christ and in communion with the Holy Spirit.

Salvation is not what I have done to get to heaven; it is what Christ has done to get me there.

Salvation is not only *from* but also *for*; *from* sin *for* participation in the life of God; *from* serving Satan *for* serving Christ; *from* disobedience to God *for* obedience.

"Salvation is like being pregnant," said John Killinger, "something has happened to you, but not everything that is going to." New life will issue from you.

Salvation is the restoration of the image of God in man. It is:

to live authentically,
to acquire the Holy Spirit,
to be a living temple of God,
to be in the Kingdom of God now,
to share in life as God created it to be,
to be by grace what God is by nature,
to achieve theosis (God in us now),
to ascend to the throne of God through prayer,
to be loved by God and accepted by Him,
to be an heir of God's Kingdom.

This is the salvation Christ offers us now.
"Sirs, what must I do to be saved?"

What must I do to receive all these blessings of salvation?

"Believe in the Lord Jesus and you will be saved . . ."

PRAYER

We have seen the true light. We have received the Holy Spirit. We have found the true faith. We worship the undivided Trinity, and *it has saved us*.. Amen. (From the Liturgy of St. John Chrysostom.)

It Is More Blessed to Give Than to Receive

Sunday of the Holy Fathers of the First Ecumenical Council (Acts 20:16-18 and 28-36)

"It is more blessed to give than to receive" (Acts 20:36).

In today's Epistle lesson St. Paul quotes words uttered by Jesus but not found in any of the four Gospels, i.e., "It is more blessed to give than to receive."

Dr. Adler, a famous psychiatrist, said, "I suppose all the ills of the human personality can be traced back to one thing, namely, not understanding the meaning of the statement (of Jesus): 'It is more blessed to give than to receive.' " Dr. Paul Tillich, a famous theologian, said once, "People are sick not only because they have not received love, but also because they are not allowed to give it." For our mental and physical health we *need* to give. "It is more blessed to give than to receive."

A child becomes an adult when he stops taking and starts giving. In fact, one of the best signs of maturity is the ability to give. "It is more blessed to give than to receive."

A child becomes an adult when he stops taking and

starts giving. In fact, one of the best signs of maturity is the ability to give. "It is more blessed to give than to receive."

There are those who rant and rave against the commercialization of Christmas and Mother's Day. I'm not one of them because anything that reminds people to express love and appreciation to one another is a blessing. "It is more blessed to give than to receive."

The Best Definition of Christianity

During a stewardship campaign a parishioner complained that Christianity is one continual give, give, give. The pastor replied, "Thank you for the finest definition of Christianity I have ever heard. Christianity is one continual give, give, give. That's the way it all began. God gave. He gave His only Son. His Son gave. He gave His life on the cross that we may have life. His disciples gave. They left their homes and businesses to devote full time to Christ as spreaders of His Good News. Most of the twelve died a martyr's death. Through the ages the work of Christ has prospered to the extent that Christians have been willing to give, give, give." "It is more blessed to give than to receive."

The Example of Jesus

Jesus taught us to give first when He gave His life for us on the cross before any of us loved Him (Romans 5:8).

He taught us to give without waiting for the other person to give first. Instead of asking, "Why doesn't that person smile at me?" He taught us to ask, "Why am I not smiling at him?" Instead of asking, "Why doesn't this person help me?" Jesus taught us to ask, "Why am I not helping him?" Instead of asking, "Why doesn't this person give to me?" Jesus invites us to ask, "Why am I not giving to him?" Jesus showed us a new and better way of life, i.e., that "it is more blessed to give than to receive."

Gifts to Give

What are some of the gifts we can be giving others?

There is the gift of encouragement, the gift of saying, "I love you" to someone whose love we have taken for granted, the gift of forgiveness, the gift of saying, "I'm sorry" to someone we have hurt, the gift of understanding, the gift of really listening when another speaks to try to get his or her point of view, to try to understand how he or she really feels. To give one's whole and serious attention to another person, is a real gift. How blessed it is to be able to give these gifts.

The Gift of Praise

All of us need praise. When we don't get it, life becomes unbearable. When we do get it, we tend to live up to it. The desire to be praised and appreciated is perhaps one of the deepest needs we have. Few gifts we can ever give are greater than praise.

At the commencement exercises upon graduation from medical school, a young man walked over to his widowed mother and placed the diploma in her hand. As he kissed her brow he said, "Mother, that's yours. You earned it. Thank you so much for all you've done for me." How blessed it is to give praise when it is due.

Give to the One in Greatest Need

The Lord Jesus tells us that whatever the gift we give,

we should give it to the person with the greatest need, expecting nothing in return: "When you give a dinner or banquet, do not invite your friends or your brothers or your kinsmen or your rich neighbors, lest they also invite you in return, and you be repaid. But when you give a feast, invite the poor, the maimed, the lame, the blind, and you will be blessed, because they cannot repay you. You will be repaid at the resurrection of the just" (St. Luke 14:12-24). One teen-age Swiss girl who wanted to buy a gift for a pastor bought a baby dress, and delivered it in person in the name of the pastor to the poorest family she could find. Here is an example of real giving as taught by our Lord Jesus. How much more blessed it is to give to the one who is in greatest need!

The Gift of Christ

Stephen Neill, in his book "The Difference in Being a Christian," says, "The greatest gift that any man can give to any other is Christ. Very few people pass even a single day without being in touch with someone who does not know Christ, and who greatly needs to know Him. Can we pretend that we love if we are not passing on the knowledge of Him?" How many parents take the time to pass on to their children the greatest gift there is: Christ, by praying with them, by having family devotions at the supper table, by reading Bible stories to them, by coming to church with them every Sunday? And how many of us take the time to invite a non-church-goer to church when we meet such a person on the street or at home? "To know Christ is life eternal," says the Bible. "In Christ," says St. Paul, "are hid all the treasures of wisdom and knowledge." Is there any gift more inexpensive to give than Christ and yet more priceless? How blessed it is to share this greatest of all gifts!

Still Other Gifts

A tramp looking for a handout said, "Can you spare a few cents for a cup of coffee?" A tightwad snapped back, "Why don't you do something useful for a living instead of begging? You need brains more than money."

The tramp replied, "Well, sir, I asked you for what I thought you had most of."

What are the gifts people need most today?

Perhaps:

—to an enemy, forgiveness.
—to those who need it, friendship.
—to those who depend on us, loyalty.
—to those with whom we come in contact, kindness.
—to those whose views may differ from ours, understanding.
—to yourself, respect.
—to all men, charity

The Gift of Self-Esteem

Another great gift we can all give is self-esteem. Whenever we help anyone raise his or her self-esteem, we are producing and giving a great gift of love.

The secretary of the Ecumenical Patriarch, Fr. Demetrios, purchased a ring one day in a bazaar in Istanbul. The proprietor of the store told some visitors from America whom Fr. Demetrios was conducting on a tour: "He cannot afford that ring. He is buying it for a little girl whose parents lost their home and business in the recent riots." Fr. Demetrios responded, "I suppose I ought to give her some shoes or a coat. But I did not want to give her a gift to remind her of her poverty. I want her to know that she is loved."

Self-esteem is one of the greatest gifts we can give anyone. A great saint cautioned his disciples to deport themselve so that "the poor will forgive you the bread you give them," he said.

One cold, rainy night an elderly lady got off a bus and asked a person at the bus stop, "When is the next bus due?"

The person asked which bus and, when she replied, he said, "But you just got off that one."

"Well," she stammered a bit shyly, "you see there was a terribly crippled young man on that bus and nobody offered him a seat. I knew he'd be embarrassed if an old lady like me got up for him, so I just pretended it was time for me to get off and I rang the bell as he came alongside my seat. He wasn't embarrassed, and I—well, there's always another bus."

How much more blessed it is to give without embarrassing the one to whom we give.

Give to God

If it is blessed to give to our fellow humans, how much more blessed must it be to give to God. But what can we give God? Does He not have everything? Is not the entire universe in His hands? But does God have everything when He has placed in our hands the one thing that cannot be commanded, and never forced—our love and allegiance?

Give God your repentance and He will give you the gift of His forgiveness. Give Him your life and He will give you the gift of meaning and purpose even in suffering, even in death. Give Him your sorrow and He will give you the gift of His peace. Give Him your emptiness and He will give you the fulness of His Presence. Give Him your despair and He will replace it with hope. Give Him your weakness and He will give you His strength. Give Him your time; He will give you His eternity. Give Him your soul and He will make it His home, His temple, His palace.

"It is more blessed to give than to receive" to man and to God.

PRAYER

O Lord,
You have taught me how to pray—
Teach me how to give.
Forgive me
If I have hurt anyone
By flinging my silver carelessly
In the face of need,
Or humiliated men
By making them victims
Of my charity.
Help me to give
Out of love,
To give myself,
To know when to give and run
And when to give and keep on giving
'Till the work is done.
Teach me how to add
The finishing touch;
And if it be Your holy will—
The hardest thing of all—
How to give
In the name
Of Christ.
Amen.

—David Redding

"And They Were Filled with the Holy Spirit"

Sunday of Pentecost (Acts 2:1-11)

"And they were filled with the Holy Spirit . . . "(Acts 2:4).

A person asked one day,
"Lord, what is Pentecost anyway?
I mean for me.
I know all about what it was then and that was great!
But what about now?
I don't want to talk in tongues,
But I do want to know that Pentecost joy and excitement.
I do want to know that sense of direction,
that sense of power,
that sense of knowing God,
that commitment to Your task
with no reservations."
Lord, what is Pentecost?

What was it then? Was it not power? Was it not life? Was it not enthusiasm? Was it not boldness in witnessing for Christ? Was it not miracles of healing? Was it not divine Wisdom? Was it not God leading and guiding His people?

Was it not excitement? Was it not joy? If that is what Pentecost was 2,000 years ago, can it not be the same today?

Why Not Today?

There are those who limit Pentecost to the past when the Church needed God's special help to spread in a hostile and pagan world. But Pentecost is not just for the past. Where there is fervent faith in Christ today, there is Pentecost. Where there is prayer, there is Pentecost. Where there are those who wait on the Lord expectantly, there is Pentecost. Where there is a real abiding in Christ through Holy Communion, there is Pentecost. And where there is Pentecost, there is power. There is life. There is wisdom. There is joy. There is praise. There is God within, guiding, upholding, overcoming, bringing good out of evil, loving, accepting, forgiving, uplifting, resurrecting.

Bishop Ignatios of Latakia wrote,

"Without the Holy Spirit, God is far away,
Christ stays in the past,
The Gospel is a dead letter
The Church is simply an organization,
prayer is merely a formality,
the liturgy an empty ritual,
Christian living a slave morality.

"But with the Holy Spirit all changes:
the cosmos is resurrected, it groans with the birthpangs of the kingdom.
The risen Christ is here,
life is pervaded by joy and priase,
The Gospel becomes a living letter from Christ,

prayer becomes a dialogue with the living God,
the liturgy comes alive with Christ,
our human acts are done in Christ and for Christ."

How Does the Holy Spirit Come?

One of the most important prayers in the Orthodox liturgy is the prayer the priest directs to God the Father for the consecration of the bread and wine into the Precious Body and Blood of Jesus: "Send Your Holy Spirit upon us and upon these Gifts." We too should be saying this prayer as we kneel at this point of the liturgy: "Father, send Your Holy Spirit upon us."

This invoking or calling upon the Holy Spirit to fill us with God's presence is called "Epiclesis" and is fundamental to all Orthodox theology and devotion. Almost every worship service in our church begins with the Epiclesis contained in the beautiful prayer: "Heavenly King, Comforter, the Spirit of truth . . . come and dwell (pitch your tent) in us."

Pentecost Then

Every year on Pentecost Sunday we kneel three times and pray three prayers which are an Epiclesis, a calling upon the Holy Spirit to "come and pitch His tent in us." For it was on this day that the Spirit came in His fulness upon the disciples filling them with the Power and Wisdom and Presence of God. When we look at the twelve disciples, we see that they were ordinary men. There was not a distinguished name among them. They were capable, respectable men, but there was no emperor or scholar, or even a clergyman, to add luster to the list. Yet when the Holy Spirit had entered them, they accomplished the most stupendous task ever undertaken by any group in human history.

Pentecost Today

Pentecost began with the Epiclesis of the Apostles as they waited upon God in prayer. Pentecost continues today with our Epiclesis, our prayer to the Holy Spirit to fill us with the fruits of the Spirit: "love, joy, peace, patience, kindness, goodness, faithfulness, gentleness, self-control" (Gal. 5:22, 27).

The same Spirit Who "moved upon the face of the waters" in the first creation and created order out of chaos comes today through our Epiclesis—our prayer—to create peace out of the turmoil and confusion of our lives.

"And Mary said to the angel, 'How can this be since I have no husband?' And the angel said to her, '*The Holy Spirit will come upon you . . .* ' " (Luke 1:34, 35). The same Spirit Who overshadowed the Theotokos and brought Christ to us at Christmas, is invoked in every liturgy and continues to bring Christ to us, changing the Gifts of bread and wine into the Precious Body and Blood of our Lord.

The same Holy Spirit Who came upon Jesus at His Baptism is invoked with the Epiclesis of the priest and comes to sanctify the "new womb" of the Church, the baptismal font, where God's children are conceived and born again of water and the Spirit.

We are—all of us—the image of God, but especially so when through our Epiclesis, we invite the Holy Spirit to "come and pitch His tent" in us.

The Christians' purpose in life is to acquire the Holy Spirit (St. Seraphim of Sarov), to be deified (St. Irenaeus), to become "partakers of divine nature" (St. Peter 1:4), to become "god by grace and adoption" (St. Symeon the New Theologian). This purpose was fulfilled on Pentecost when the Holy Spirit came to abide in us in His fulness. "And they were filled with the Holy Spirit. . . . "

Pentecost Through Prayer

But Pentecost is now. Pentecost is today and every day. For Pentecost happens whenever we pray the Epiclesis, " . . . Spirit of Truth . . . come and pitch your tent in us." "Every virtuous act done for Christ's sake gives us the grace of the Holy Spirit," said St. Seraphim of Sarov, "but most of all is this given through prayer; for prayer is always in our hands as an instrument for acquiring the grace of the Holy Spirit." *"And they were filled with the Holy Spirit . . . "*

"I will pour out my Spirit upon all flesh, and your sons and daughters shall prophesy and your young men shall see visions, and your old men shall dream dreams . . . " (Acts 2:17).

Pentecost in Every Liturgy

The Spirit was poured out on us at Pentecost. He continues to be poured out on us today through the Epiclesis. It was with the Epiclesis that the Church was built up. It is the Epiclesis which makes those who partake of the Precious Body and Blood into the "soma pneumatikon"—the spiritual body of the Lord. It is after we have prayed the Epiclesis of the liturgy that the Holy Spirit comes upon us and permits us to sing at the end, "We have seen the true light. *We have received the Heavenly Spirit.* We have found the true faith." Pentecost happens again in every liturgy. *"And they were filled with the Holy Spirit . . . "* And so are we today!

If the inner man is not filled with the Spirit of God, it will be filled with evil spirits that are just waiting to rush in and fill the emptiness. But as long as the inner emptiness is filled with the Holy Spirit, there will be no room for demonic spirits.

Pentecost Every Day

Prayer for the Orthodox Christian is a perpetual Epiclesis. Many times each day we are called to pray, "Spirit of truth . . . come and pitch your tent in us." When we wake in the morning, when we retire in the evening, when we are anxious and fearful, when we seek guidance, we pray: "Heavenly King, Comforter, Spirit of truth . . . come and pitch your tent in us. Guide us. Inspire us. Strengthen us. Without You we are nothing. With You rivers of living water shall flow out of our hearts."

Trying to excuse himself for a failure to do what was right, a person said, "I couldn't help it. You can't imagine the pressure I was up against." His friend replied, "Yes, but where were your inner braces?" The inner brace is always the Spirit of God. *"And they were filled with the Holy Spirit . . . "*

Today we are going to ask all of you to perform an experiment. We are going to ask you to *take Pentecost home with you.* For this next week, as you pray every day, include a request to the Holy Spirit that He fill you with God's presence and power; that He lead you and show you the way to go; that He come and dwell in your heart. Pray this fervently and faithfully every day and discover for yourself what this added dimension of the third Person of the Godhead can do for you. For Christianity is not just talk; it is power—a power that comes from the presence of the Holy Spirit within.

There is a vast difference between having food on your plate beside you and having that food inside your stomach where it can nourish you and help you grow. Take God within you today! Receive the Holy Spirit! "And they were filled with the Holy Spirit . . . "

PRAYER

"Come, Holy Spirit, come!
Come like the fire and burn;
Come like the wind and cleanse;
Come like the light and reveal.
Come pitch your tent in us.
Convict. Convert. Consecrate.
Until we are wholly thine. Amen."

* * * * *

"O Heavenly King, the Paraclate,
The ever-present Spirit of Truth,
Who fills all Creation,
The Treasure of all good things,
The Giver of Life;
Come and dwell among us;
And cleanse us from all sin;
And save our souls,
Thou Good and Holy Spirit."

Get Rid of the Barnacles!

The Sunday of All Saints (Hebrews 11:33-12:2)

". . . let us lay aside every weight and sin which clings so closely, and let us run with perseverance the race that is set before us" (Hebrews 12:1).

Barnacles that accumulate on the bottom of ships are a multimillion dollar headache for shipowners. No bigger than walnuts, they can slow down a ship weighing thousands of tons. Within six months after it goes into the water, a vessel may acquire 2 or 3 inches of these barnacles. The layer can weigh 100 tons and reduce a ship's speed by more than ten percent.

A one-inch growth of barnacles on the bottom of a super-tanker can create an underwater drag that adds as much as $114,000 of extra fuel consumption during a year's time.

Watching workmen sandblast the heavily barnacled hull of a dry-docked tanker, the captain of the ship said, "They'll probably remove about fifteen tons of marine growth—mostly barnacles—from that one ship. And it's been less than two years since her last scrub-down. The drag caused by only a six-month accumulation can force a vessel to burn 40% more fuel just to maintain normal cruising speed."

A navy admiral said, "We can't afford to carry much extra fuel on combat missions. Any loss of speed makes us more vulnerable to attack. Also, if we release a ship from a battle zone for cleaning, we reduce our firepower.

"Then, too, friction from hitchhiking barnacles can make an otherwise quiet ship into a noisy one, more easily detected by listening devices. Even one barnacle, clinging to a sonar dome can seriously distort echolocation."

The only way to get rid of the pesty barnacle is to haul the vessel out of the water and scrape them off—often with a jackhammer. For idle hours in port plus clean-up charges, the cost to world-wide shipping interests comes to several billions of dollars a year.

Barnacles in Our Lives

Like ships, we human beings can also accumulate barnacles that slow us down and burden us with unnecessary drag. St. Paul talks about this in today's Epistle lesson when he says, " . . . let us lay aside every weight and sin which clings so closely, and let us run with perseverance the race that is set before us . . . " (Hebrews 12:1).

Life for Paul was a race to be run and a crown to be won. In that race, sin that "clings so closely," is like a barnacle, an extra weight that slows us down. He calls us on to "cast aside" every such "weight and sin."

Kinds of Barnacles

Consider for a moment the kinds of barnacles that accumulate in our lives.

There are the barnacles of anxiety that slow us down

in the race of life by depriving us of the serenity that should be ours as we live one day at a time and trust Jesus completely for all our needs.

There are the barnacles of bitterness that some people allow to cling to their sides—and insides—filling them with poisonous thoughts that deprive them of valuable peace of mind.

There are the barnacles of past sins that cling to us. Instead of claiming Christ's forgiveness for them, we brood over them and let them drag us down and knock us out.

There are the barnacles of discouragement that make us look at life through the dark glasses of despair and hopelessness robbing us of the joy and happiness that should be ours as children of God.

There are the barnacles of unbelief that cling to our eyes like scales and prevent us from seeing God and the true values in life. There were the "barnacles" that had accumulated on Paul's eyes. Suddenly, on the road to Damascus, these scales fell from his eyes, and it was like seeing for the first time. It was like living for the first time. It was like being born again into a new life. It was like giving up everything that had looked good and finding what was really good.

There are the barnacles of resentment that weigh us down terribly by destroying our poise and tranquility.

There are the barnacles of pride, envy, greed, slothfulness. St. Paul gives us a whole list of barnacles. He calls them "the works of the flesh." We read in Galatians 5:19-21, "Now the works of the flesh are plain: immorality, impurity, licentiousness, idolatry, sorcery, enmity, strife, jealousy, anger, selfishness, dissension, party spirit, envy, drunkenness, carousing, and the like.

I warn you, as I warned you before, that those who do such things shall not inherit the kingdom of God."

How to Remove Barnacles

How do we remove the weight of sin, the annoying barnacles that accumulate in our lives?

As it is not an easy task with ships, so it is not an easy task for us. St. Paul likens it to a crucifixion: "And those who belong to Christ have crucified the flesh with its passions and desires" (Gal. 5:24).

Jesus speaks of the spiritual surgery that is required in order to remove the barnacles of sin: "If your right eye causes you to sin, pluck it out and throw it away; it is better that you lose one of your members than that your whole body be thrown into hell. And if your right hand causes you to sin, cut it off and throw it away; it is better that you lose one of your members than that your whole body go into hell" (Matt. 5:29-30). Jesus, of course, is not speaking literally here. He doesn't want us to start dismembering our bodies. But He is using strong language to impress on us the necessity of removing from our lives anything that hinders us, weighs us down, and impedes us in running the race and winning the prize.

By far the best way to keep our lives free of the barnacles of sin is by coming to Jesus daily and letting Him scrape us clean of every "weight" and "sin" through heartfelt repentance and honest confession. He alone can make us clean and present us before God, justified.

Looking to Jesus

As we run the race of life we keep Jesus in full view at all times, looking to Him the pioneer and perfector of our faith. To use the words of St. Paul in today's Epistle lesson:

"Therefore, since we are surrounded by so great a cloud of witnesses, let us also lay aside every weight and sin which clings so closely, and let us run with perseverance the race that is set before us, looking to Jesus the pioneer and perfector of our faith, who for the joy that was set before Him endured the cross, despising the shame, and is seated at the right hand of the throne of God" (Hebrews 12:1-2).

There is a race to run and a prize to be won. Get rid of the barnacles!

PRAYER

Lord, all of us have barnacles. Most of us are unable to see them because of the devil who blinds us. But we feel the drag in our spiritual life. We know they are there. Help us to acknowledge their existence, Lord, and to bring them to You in honest confession. Cleanse us as we head for the goal of our high calling. Amen.

A Conscience That Bears Witness to God

Second Sunday of Matthew (Romans 2:10-16)

"They show that what the law requires is written on their hearts, while their conscience also bears witness. . . ." (Romans 2:15).

A frightened little boy asked his mother one day, "Mother, I was going to do something wrong and I heard a voice inside me say, 'You must not do it. You must not do it.' Mother, what is that voice?"

The mother replied, "Son, that is the voice of God speaking in your heart. If you listen to it and obey it, it will grow louder and louder as the years go on, and it will tell you the right thing to do. But if you disobey it, it will grow softer and softer until finally it will fade out and die. In the end you will find yourself in the dark with no one to help you and no one to lead you."

In his prayer that night the little boy was heard to say, "Oh, God, please keep that voice loud!"

What is that inner voice in each one of us called conscience?

God's Basis for Judgment

In today's Epistle lesson Paul talks about conscience. He attempts to answer the question of how God will judge those who had no opportunity to hear about Christ. He gives the Christian answer. God is fair, he says. He will not hold a man responsible for what he does not know. He will judge a man on the basis of how faithful he was to the highest he knew. For the Jew this meant the written law; for the Gentile it meant the unwritten law in his heart; the voice of conscience. Paul's argument is that in the very nature of man there is implanted an instinctive knowledge of right and wrong.

A Beam of Divine Light

Airplanes are guided into airports by means of a radio beam. The beam is a path of radio waves emanating from the airport. When the plane veers off the beam to the right, for example, the pilot gets a dash and dot signal. When he veers to the left, he gets a dot and dash signal. When he is directly on the beam he hears a constant hum. This is how the plane finds its way to the airport in bad weather.

Even more marvelous than this, however, is the fact that within the breast of every person there is a beam of divine light, called conscience, emanating from God and guiding us to Him Who is our Peace and Joy. No wonder Immanuel Kant said once that there were just two things in the universe that filled him with awe—the starry heavens above and the voice of conscience within.

A Part of the Image of God

Nicolas Berdyaev wrote of conscience, "Conscience . . . is connected with the very essence of man, with the divine image and likeness in him . . . (it) is remembrance of God and of the divine life . . . it is the organ whereby we become aware of God . . . *Conscience is the memory of what man really is, of the world to which he ideally belongs, of his Creator, of the purpose for which he has been created.*

" *

Its Origin and Purpose

How did conscience originate? There are those who say that conscience has nothing to do with God; it is social in origin. It is something that has come to us through tradition and tribal customs. Berdyaev replies to this, "Conscience is the spiritual, supernatural principle in man and *it is not of social origin at all.* It is rather the perversion and confusion of conscience that is of social origin." * The Fathers of the Church clearly state that conscience is not something acquired but is a distinct power (dynamis) *implanted in the soul by God.* It is part of the image of God in man.

Everything in the universe has something *implanted* in its nature by God to help it attain the purpose for which it was created. In chemicals, it is the law of valence which causes chemicals to combine in exactly the same way everywhere in the universe. In the plant kingdom, it is the law of metabolism which causes the acorn to grow into an oak tree and not an evergreen. In animals, it is the law of instinct. In man, the masterpiece of God's creation, it is the law of conscience that guides him to attain the exalted purpose for which he was created.

---

* "The Destiny of Man," Nicolas Berdyaev. Charles Scribner, N.Y.

Anne Morrow Lindberg wrote in her book "The Steep Ascent," "People died all the time in their lives. Parts of them died when they made the wrong kind of decisions—decisions against life . . . but you always knew when you made a decision against life. When you denied life you were warned. The cock crowed, always, somewhere inside of you."

A Warning Bell

Southey once wrote a poem entitled "The Inchcape Rock" wherein he tells of the abbott of a monastery who placed a bell on a dangerous rock to warn incoming vessels. A roving pirate once sacked the town and cast the bell into the sea. Years later, on a wild and stormy night, this same pirate tried to steer his way into the same harbor. But he listened in vain for the bell which would have given him his bearings, and he and his ship went down.

How much this reminds us of Paul's words to Timothy, "By rejecting conscience, certain persons have made shipwreck of their faith. . . ." (I Timothy 1:10). When the divine warning bell of conscience is silenced, there cannot but be a shipwreck of faith and life.

A Merciless Accuser

When conscience acts as an accuser, it is merciless. St. John Chrysostom said once that "he who lives in wickedness experiences the torments of hell prior to hell, being stung by his conscience." St. Gregory of Nyssa said, "Nothing weighs down on the soul and depresses it as conscience of sin." And one of the hymns of the Orthodox Church says in part, "Hence I have been censured, hence I the wretch have been condemned by my own conscience, than which nothing in the world is more violent." Nicolas Berdyaev wrote, "The most pitiless tribunal is that of one's own conscience; it brings with it torments of hell."

In Edgar Allen Poe's story, "Telltale Heart," the murderer buried the body of his victim in the basement. No one looked for it there. No one knew it was there *but he knew.* And that was enough. He could hear the heart of the person he had murdered beating under the floor. The beat grew louder and louder until he thought everyone could hear. In reality, of course, it was not the heart of his victim but his own conscience beating, reminding him of his sin.

An Augusta, Georgia, woman came to the police one day and confessed the "perfect murder." She had killed her roommate three years before. Who condemned her? Who judged her? Who led her to pick up the phone and call the police? Conscience! She couldn't stand it anymore. She just couldn't live with herself.

"Cleanse the Stuffed Bosom"

An accusing conscience can produce physical and mental illness. The murder of Duncan, for example, produced this kind of illness in Lady MacBeth. When Macbeth asked the physician about her illness, he replied:

"Not so sick, my Lord,
As she is troubled with thick-coming fancies,
That keep her from the rest."

The doctor was then asked a question that many physicians are asked today:

"Canst thou not minister to a mind diseased,
Pluck from the memory a rooted sorrow,
Raze out the written troubles of the brain,
And with some sweet oblivious antidote

Cleanse the stuff'd bosom of that perilous stuff
Which weighs upon the heart?" (Macbeth).

No earthly physician can "cleanse the stuff'd bosom of that perilous stuff that weighs upon the heart" and makes life a nightmare. Only one Physician can do that—the heavenly Physician. Only He can cleanse conscience, and bring it to the "peace of God that passes all understanding."

PRAYER

Lord, sin wreaks havoc with my conscience.
The pain of guilt makes me experience hell
before hell. Today I bring my sins and guilt
to you, my Great Sin-Bearer and Savior.
Remove these intolerably heavy burdens,
Lord, and restore to my conscience
Your peace that I may experience heaven before heaven.
Amen.

God Shows His Love for Us

The Third Sunday of Matthew (Romans 5:1-10)

"God shows His love for us in that while we were yet sinners Christ died for us" (Romans 5:8).

God loved us while we were yet sinners. That is what makes God's love so wonderful. He didn't wait until we had reformed and mended our ways before He loved us. He didn't wait until we loved Him before He loved us. He loved us while we still spurned and rejected His love. He still does.

Sinners Who Are Loved

"I hate myself. I am a no good sinner. I am a nothing and a nobody." Such expressions of self-contempt are often heard; and sometimes they are most loudly expressed by Christians.

But we Christians should know better. " . . . while we were yet sinners Christ died for us." We are sinners—but sinners who are loved; sinners for whom Christ died; sinners whom God so loved that He gave His only Son that we who believe in Him may not perish but have life everlasting. Therefore to hate ourselves is to hate what God loves. And this is not a sign of deep piety but of unbelief. Moreover, so long as we think of our own unworthiness, we will be too occupied with ourselves to get on with what God has put us here to do: to love Him and our neighbors as ourselves.

If I want to be a Christian, I will not forget all the things that are wrong with me, but, after that, I will add: but God nevertheless loves me. Therefore, I can accept myself—and love others as I have been loved.

Hate the Sin—Love the Sinner

The main theme of Haim Ginott's best seller, BETWEEN PARENT AND CHILD, can be summarized in a few sentences. Ginott says that parents must make the distinction between correcting a child for wrong behavior and belittling him as a person. It's the difference between a parent saying to a child, "The thing you did was wrong and I will not stand for that, because I love you too much to allow you to grow up with that kind of behavior," and saying to the child, "You are a terrible person because you did such a thing."

You can easily see the difference—correcting and disciplining bad behavior, but never belittling the personhood of a child, never rejecting him or withdrawing your love from him as a person.

When you summarize this, what do you have? You have the basic biblical truth: hate the sin but love the sinner. This is the way God loves us:

"God shows His love for us in that while we were yet sinners Christ died for us." God hates the sin but never withdraws His love from the sinner.

What Makes Us Lovable

Ruel Howe said once, "We are not loved because we

are lovable but we can become lovable because we are loved. It is precisely when my children need to be loved that I find them so unlovable." Why did God *love* Moses or David or Paul or Zacchaeus? Did He love them because of their goodness? Certainly not! They were all sinners. Moses was a murderer. David was a murderer and adulterer. Paul was a persecutor of Christians. Zacchaeus was a dishonest tax collector. It was because God loved them in spite of their sins that they became saints. "Name one harlot," someone asked, "who has ever been reclaimed by being treated as a harlot." Christ loved harlots and murderers and thieves and adulterers. It was to save them that He shed His precious blood. It was the transforming power of His love that made these people new persons—the same love that can make us new persons.

Perhaps there is a lesson for us here. If we who were loved by God when we were unlovable, can apply this same kind of love to other unlovable people, perhaps we will be giving them that which they need most if they are to find God and themselves: love.

So when the devil comes to us and tempts us with the thought, "How could God love me? I have been immoral, I have lied, I have stolen, have even committed murder—no, God could never love me," remind the tempter of other sinners before you, like Moses, David, Paul, Zacchaeus; take him to the cross, and confront him with the words of Romans 5:8, "God shows His love for us in that while we were yet sinners Christ died for us." Christ did not die for saints. He died for sinners to make them saints.

He didn't wait for us to mend our ways before He loved us.

He didn't wait for us to love Him before He loved us.

He hates sin but loves the sinner.

He knows we're sinners but does not withdraw His love from us. He pleads with us to come to Him for forgiveness and new life.

He shows His love by dying for us while we were yet sinners.

PRAYER

Dear Lord, to know oneself loved and forgiven at so terrible a cost brings us to our knees in utter penitence. Set us upon our feet again, Lord, ready for Your command. Amen.

Created for Good Works

Sunday of the Holy Fathers (Titus 3:8-15)

". . . those who believe in God may be careful to apply themselves to good deeds; these are excellent and profitable to men" (Titus 3:8).

"And let our people learn to apply themselves to good deeds, so as to help cases of urgent need, and not to be unfruitful" (Titus 3:14).

A pastor who had an honorary Doctor of Divinity degree had a son who had just received an M.D. degree. One day the phone rang. A person asked to speak to Dr. Johnson. The wife who answered the phone asked, "Which Dr. Johnson do you want—the one who preaches or the one who practices?"

A Christian is one who not only preaches but also practices. In today's Epistle lesson St. Paul calls on us to practice what we preach. He talks about good deeds. "I desire you to insist on these things, so that those who have believed in God may be careful to apply themselves to good deeds; these are excellent and profitable to men . . . And let our people learn to apply themselves to good deeds, so as to help cases of urgent need, and not to be unfruitful" (Titus 3:8, 14). Our faith in Christ, which is invisible, is made visible through love, specifically through the good deeds that are born of love.

Created for Good Works

Paul writes in Ephesians 2:10, "For we are His workmanship, created in Christ Jesus for good works, which God prepared beforehand, that we should walk in them." This verse seems to contradict the one just before it: "For by grace you have been saved through faith; and this is not your own doing, it is the gift of God—not because of works lest any man should boast" (Ephesians 2:8-9). One verse says: "You have been saved . . . not because of works," and the next says: "Created in Christ Jesus for good works."

A New Creation Produces New Works

Far from contradicting each other, these verses give us the Christian position concerning good works. Good works do not produce salvation, but salvation produces good works. We are not saved *because* of good works, but we are saved *for* good works. Christ makes each one of us a new creation, a new being. The new being, through the power of the indwelling Christ and the Holy Spirit, produces new works. Christ does not begin by changing our deeds. He begins by changing us. The good deeds flow by God's grace out of the new person.

The Vine Dresser Looks for Fruit

The vine dresser looks for fruit. The branches are attached to the vine not just to look pretty; they are to be productive. So we, the branches, are attached to Christ, Who is our Vine, in order to produce the fruit of good works. "I am the vine, you are the branches. He who abides in me, and I in him, he it is that bears much fruit, for apart from me you can do nothing" (John 15:5). We are created for good works.

Faith Working Through Love

The person who has accepted Christ and received the Holy Spirit begins a new life which is expressed in love through good deeds. A person is not saved by faith alone but by faith which expresses itself through love as St. Paul writes. St. James asks, "What does it profit, my brethren, if a man says he has faith but has not works? Can his faith save him? If a brother or sister is ill-clad and in lack of daily food, and one of you says to them, 'Go in peace, be warmed and filled,' without giving them the things needed for the body, what does it profit? So faith by itself, if it has no works, is dead" (James 2:14-17).

Not Meritorious

The good works that we do, do not earn us any special merit points in heaven. We can never buy God's love with them since Jesus specifically tells us: "So you also, when you have done all that is commanded you, say, 'We are unworthy servants; we have only done what was our duty' " (Luke 17:10).

Our good deeds do not put God in our debt. It is God's love in Christ that puts us forever in His debt. Our good deeds are a feeble attempt on our part to show appreciation to God for what He has done for us. We can never succeed but neither can we stop trying. Love will not let us. "The love of Christ controls us," says Paul (2 Cor. 5:14).

Counterfeit Works

Only those good works that are done in the name of Christ are the fruit of the Holy Spirit. Good deeds—even the best—are worthless in a person who does not believe in Christ. A work is good only in so far as it is done in Christ and by the power of the Holy Spirit. For the Christian there is no good work apart from this.

A story is told of a ten-dollar bill that got into circulation and did a lot of good. It helped buy coal for a needy old woman; it helped buy medicine for a sick child, and even showed up in the collection plate in church one Sunday morning. Then it fell into the hands of a bank teller who spotted it immediately as counterfeit. The test is not how many good deeds we claim to our credit, but rather, can they pass inspection in the sight of God? Were our good deeds done in Christ and for Christ? Or are they products of pride: trying to parade our goodness or to buy God's favor and place Him in our debt?

We are created for those good works that are done in Christ and for Christ. All others are counterfeit; they cannot pass inspection in God's sight.

A Showplace of Good Deeds

The early Church was a showplace of good works done for Christ. Having been made a new creation in Christ, those early Christians began to produce new deeds that astounded the pagan world.

In one of the earliest apologetic works preserved, Justin the Martyr (d. 165), writes:

> "We used to value above all else money and possessions; now we bring together all that we have

> and share it with those who are in need (cf. Acts 4:34-37). Formerly we hated and killed one another and, because of a difference in nationality or custom, we refused to admit strangers within our gates. Now since the coming of Christ, we all live in peace. We pray for our enemies and seek to convert those who hate us unjustly . . ." (I Apology XIV).

Tertullian (160-220) said: "It is our care for the helpless, our practice of lovingkindness, that brands us in the eyes of many of our opponents. 'Only look,' they say, 'look how they love one another' " (Apology XXXIX).

"And let our people learn to apply themselves to good deeds, so as to help cases of urgent need, and not to be unfruitful." These words of Paul in today's Epistle lesson found eager expression in the lives of the early Christians who as we see from the history of the early Church:

1. gave alms to help the destitute (even poor Christians were urged to give through fasting);
2. supported widows and orphans;
3. supported the sick, the infirm, the poor, and the disabled (even establishing hospitals in many cities);
4. cared for prisoners and slaves;
5. found work for those who were unemployed;
6. cared for those who journeyed;
7. cared for the victims of great calamities. Eusebius (IX:8) writes this about Christians when a great plague struck:

> "Alone, in the midst of this terrible calamity they (the Christians) proved by visible deeds their sympathy and humanity. All day long some

> continued without rest to tend the dying and bury them—the number was immense; and there was no one to see to them; others rounded up the huge numbers who had been reduced to scarecrows all over the city and distributed loaves to them all, so that their praises were sung on every side, and all men glorified the God of the Christians and owned that they alone were pious and truly religious: did not their actions speak for themselves?"

Look about you today. Do you see anyone who is poverty-stricken, or ignored, or oppressed, or condemned to loneliness, or in despair, or hopeless? Here is your chance to do your good deed, to share with others the love of Christ!

Remember how Jesus described His mission? Good news to the poor. Release to the captives. Recovery of sight to the blind. Liberty for the oppressed. The good deeds of God's love!

If we remain attached to Christ Who is our vine, our lives as Christians will be adorned with the fruit of many good deeds. Then the promise of Christ will be fulfilled in each one of us: "Let your light so shine before men that they may *see your good works* and give glory to your Father Who is in heaven" (Matt. 5:16).

PRAYER

Blessed Jesus, help us to abide in You that we may "learn to apply ourselves to good deeds, so as to help cases of urgent need, and not be unfruitful," ever remembering that as You said, "Not one cup of cold water given in Your Name will lose its reward," remembering also that when You come again to judge the living and the dead, You will judge us on the basis of our deeds: "I was sick and you visited me; I was hungry and you fed me; I was naked and you clothed me." Amen.

What Is in the Heart Will Be on the Lips

Fifth Sunday of Matthew (Romans 10:1-10)

". . . if you confess with your lips that Jesus is Lord and believe in your heart that God raised him from the dead, you will be saved. For man believes with his heart and so is justified, and he confesses with his lips and so is saved" (Romans 10:9-10).

Whatever you believe with your heart, you will confess with your lips. If you're a young man and love a young woman with all your heart, you will stand before God's altar and confess your love for her before God and man. You will join your life with hers and become one.

What is in the heart will be on the lips. It is not otherwise with Jesus. Paul says in today's Epistle lesson: ". . . if you confess with your lips that Jesus is Lord and believe in your heart that God raised him from the dead, you will be saved." Jesus put it this way: "So every one who acknowledges me before men, I also will acknowledge before my Father who is in heaven; but whoever denies me before men, I also will deny before my Father who is in heaven" (Matthew 10:32-33).

Our Business as Christians

"Whoever shall confess me before men." It is our business as Christians to confess not ourselves, for we are hardly the center of the universe, and besides there are so many selves in us that expressing them might easily create bedlam. Our real job is to confess Christ and to become what the New Testament calls "witnesses of the Resurrection" (Acts 1:22).

Peter's Confession

One day Jesus asked His disciples: "Who do you say I am?" Peter replied, "You are the Christ, the Son of the Living God" (Matt. 18:16). Peter confessed publicly with his lips what was in his heart. It was in response to this beautiful confession of Christ's divinity that Jesus said to Peter, "You are Peter, and on this rock I will build my church, and the powers of death shall not prevail against it. I will give you the keys to the kingdom of heaven . . . " (Matt. 18:18-19). Commenting on these words Origen in the early Church said, "If we also say, 'You are the Christ, the Son of the Living God,' then we also become Peter . . . for whoever believes in Christ (as Peter did) becomes a rock. Does Christ give the keys to the kingdom to Peter alone, whereas other blessed people cannot receive them?" According to Origen, Peter is no more than the first believer and confessor of Christ. If others wish to receive the same keys, they must imitate Peter, making the same confession of faith he did: "You are the Christ, the Son of the Living God." It is not upon one person—Peter—that the Church is built but upon Peter's bold confession of faith in Jesus. " . . . if you confess with your lips that Jesus is Lord and believe in your heart that God raised him from the dead, you will be saved" (Rom. 10:9).

Eleven Million Confessors

Eleven million Christians were put to death in the early Church for no other reason than confessing Christ before men. Let me mention just one incident from Diocletian's persecution of the early Christians. A little group of Christians was attending liturgy in one of the catacombs. Among many, a father and son were taken before the Roman tribune. The father was ordered to renounce his Christian faith or pay the penalty with his life.

"Not for you or all the riches of imperial Rome," he replied, "will I deny my Savior, Jesus Christ."

Whereupon he was beheaded. When the son saw what had happened to his father he weakened.

"Be wiser than your father," said the tribune, "Deny this crucified Christ. Place a few grains of incense upon the fires burning before the gods of Rome and I will not only spare your life but give you anything you ask."

Relieved, the boy started toward the idols. He had taken about a dozen steps when he suddenly stopped. His father's words echoed in his ears. Quickly he walked over to the place where the sand was still crimson with his father's blood. He rubbed the moist sand in his hands.

"A few moments ago," he said, "I was weak and about to yield. But now I am strong with the blood of my father, and I too will die rather than deny my God."

Quickly the executioner did his job, and the blood of the son mingled with the blood of his father. "If you confess with your lips that Jesus is Lord and believe in your heart that God raised him from the dead, you will be saved." This father and son were only two of eleven million martyr-confessors in the early Church. They believed. They confessed. They were saved.

Does My Confession Show in My Life?

To confess Christ before men was originally connected with martyrdom. It cost your life to confess with your lips the Christ who was in your heart. Today we confess Jesus before men publicly every time we recite the Nicene Creed in the liturgy: "I believe . . . in one Lord Jesus Christ . . . " But are we confessing Him in our lives, at our home, at our business? If it were a crime to be a Christian, would there be enough evidence to convict us?

A group of thieves accosted a nun with the new look. She was wearing ordinary street clothes. They forced her into a car. She kept protesting, "I'm a nun." They didn't believer her. "Call the mother superior at my convent," she insisted. They did, and discovered that she was indeed speaking the truth. Before they left her, however, they stripped her back and carved a cross on it with a knife. "Next time wear something so that people will know who you are," they said to her.

Do people know who we are? Does my life confess Christ before men? Does my family know what I stand for? Do I ever confess to them with my lips the faith I have in my heart? Am I ashamed of my Savior? Do I hide my faith in Him and, like a chameleon, blend in with the colors of the sinful world around me? If so, then I need to heed the words of my Savior: "For whoever is ashamed of me and of my words in this adulterous and sinful generation, of him will the Son of man also be ashamed, when he comes in the glory of his Father with the holy angels" (Mark 8:38).

How to Confess Christ Today

How can I confess Christ today? A witness can testify only to what he himself has seen and heard; all else is hearsay and is not accepted in court. Let me share with you the experience of one person who served as a witness in court.

"I had to serve once as a witness in a court trial dealing with an automobile accident. I was scared and really didn't want to do it. I felt as if I had to convince the judge, the jury, and the insurance company that the driver was observing all the traffic laws, doing nothing wrong. Finally, it dawned on me that all they wanted from me was what I had seen and heard—what I had witnessed! That was a relief. I didn't have to prove anything. I didn't have to accomplish anything: 'Just tell the jury what you saw . . . ' Would you believe I actually enjoyed the experience? The court could do with my story what they pleased—I just told it as I saw it!"

Our job is to confess Christ by sharing what we have seen the Lord do in our lives. This is what the blind man did who had been healed by Jesus. He simply stated what Jesus did for him: " . . . one thing I know, that though I was blind, now I see" (John 9:25). For example, you fall into a conversation with a neighbor, coworker, or stranger. They, not you, bring up a problem or concern. As they talk, you remember how God helped you with one of your own problems. If you share your experience, you may fumble with words or even blush. You may come away certain that you have made a grievous mistake by sharing. But the outcome of your sharing is not up to you. It is the Lord's job to take your witness, however grand, or simple or weak, and use it to get to the heart of the one hearing you; to get him to connect with the Source of Power that will help him also, as it helped us. Who can tell what it might mean to others if we quietly testified what the Lord did for us in time of sorrow? Believe in your heart that God raised Jesus from the dead, and confess with your lips that Jesus is Lord and you will be saved—and God will even use your words to lead others to Him.

Confessing Christ Strengthens Faith

We are greatly strengthened when we make a public confession of faith in Jesus. Our faith is tremendously fortified by such an act. Try it! Say to a member of your family, "You know, one of the most precious persons in my life is the Lord Jesus. I simply cannot tell you what He has meant to me in my life—how He leads me, and guides me, and enriches my life every day." Just a simple confession, but how greatly it strengthens your faith when you say it with your lips. You will actually feel your faith growing stronger within you. Or take another example: you meet someone who does not come to church and you confess Christ by saying, "You know, I simply cannot tell you how much guidance and strength I receive in church every Sunday. Why, I can hardly wait for Sunday morning to come along. Mind if I pick you up next Sunday and we worship together?" Not only will your faith grow stronger when you confess Jesus this way, but you have His word for it that He will not forget it: one day He will "acknowledge you before His Father in heaven."

John Berryman wrote a poem in which he recalls how boldly the martyrs of the early church confessed their faith in Christ. He looks at his own life and thinks of the many things that can happen to him before the end comes. He prays that no matter what happens his lips may be ready to confess his Lord: "Cancer, senility, mania, I pray I may be ready with my witness."

" . . . if you confess with your lips that Jesus is Lord and believe in your heart that God raised Him from the dead, you will be saved."

PRAYER

Blessed Jesus, You are in my heart. May my lips confess boldly Your Presence within me that the world may come to know You through my humble confession. It is in confessing You as Lord with my lips and believing in my heart that God raised You from the dead that I shall be saved. All praise and glory be to You together with the Father and the Holy Spirit. Amen.

Outdo One Another in Showing Honor

Sixth Sunday of Matthew (Romans 12:614)

"Outdo one another in showing honor" (Romans 12:10)

The ancient Greeks had a story of a Spartan called Paedaretos. Three hundred men were to be chosen to govern Sparta and Paedaretos was a candidate. When the list of the successful was announced, his name was not on it. "I am sorry," said one of his friends, "that you were not elected. The people ought to have known what a wise officer of state you would have made." "I am glad," said Paedaretos, "that in Sparta there are three hundred men better than I am."

Here was a man who became a legend because he was prepared to give to others the first place and to bear no ill will.

To many people, the most important thing in life is to have a front seat, to be sought after. The aim of a Christian, on the other hand, is never to place himself on display or to be concerned with his own interests. St. Paul expressed it this way: "Do nothing from selfishness or conceit, but in humility count others better than yourselves" (Phil. 2:3). One translator of this verse expressed it this way: "Practice treating one another as your superiors." To be so mature in Christ that one does not have to feel superior to anyone—that is the test of a growing Christian. St. Paul expressed the same truth this way in today's Epistle lesson: "Outdo one another in showing honor."

The Humble Abbot

There is a story of a monk, a very holy man, who was sent to take up office as abbot (head) of a monastery. He looked so humble a person that, when he arrived, he was sent to work in the kitchen as a scullion, because no one recognized him. Without a word of protest, and with no attempt to assert his authority, he washed dishes and did the most menial tasks. It was only when the bishop arrived a considerable time later that the mistake was discovered and the humble monk took up his true position as head of the monastery. "Outdo one another in showing honor."

Goethe and Schiller

In the city of Weimar, Germany, there is a statue of Goethe and Schiller, two great poets. The German people like to see the plays of these two poets performed in the theatre and they invariably compare them asking, "Which one is the greater?"

Schiller and Goethe were friends. They met together frequently and enjoyed talking to each other. If Goethe heard people say, "Sir, you are the master poet of the Germans," he was quick to reply, "But do not forget

Schiller." And Schiller would always say the same about Goethe.

The sculptor of the statue of Weimar expressed their mutual friendship beautifully. He has put a wreath of laurel leaves in Goethe's hand. The poet is raising his hand to place the wreath on his friend Schiller's head. But Schiller does not wish for the crown, which he thinks Goethe deserves more. He is thrusting it back, as if saying, "No, it is more fit for you to wear than me." Thus, the two friends nobly disagreed, each refusing to be crowned. But in their hearts they loved one another, appreciating each other's qualities. "Outdo one another in showing honor."

The Naval Officer's Promotion

A young naval officer kept his promotion to lieutenant-commander a secret, until he got his new gold-leaf collar insignia. He walked into his home and waited proudly for his wife to notice the insignia of his promotion. An hour passed and she said nothing. He was quite disappointed. But then he noticed that she was on the verge of tears. He put his arms around her and asked what was wrong. "You didn't even notice my new hair-do!" she sobbed.

It is this preoccupation with self that causes so much distress in life. We need the love of Jesus which thinks more of the happiness of others than it thinks of its own; the love that is proud to serve; the love that outdoes others in showing honor; the Christlike love which knows that in forgetting self it will find self, and that in losing itself it will fulfill itself.

"Jesus . . . did not count equality with God a thing to be grasped, but *emptied himself*, taking the form of a servant . . . He . . . became obedient unto death, even death on a cross" (Phil. 2:6-8). He Who is God willingly suffered all this humiliation, this dethronement from His position as Lord of the universe, this slashing of His pride to bring about our salvation. He outdid others in showing us honor and love.

For, what greater honor is there than to have the Son of God lay down His life for us?

PRAYER

Come Holy Spirit, make your home in us. Give us the great fruit of love which outdoes others in showing honor. Amen.

The Encouragement of the Scriptures

Seventh Sunday of Matthew (Romans 15:1-7)

"For whatever was written in former days was written for our instruction, that by steadfastness and by the encouragement of the scriptures we might have hope" (Romans 15:4).

The Apostle Paul tells us in today's Epistle lesson that by the encouragement of the Scriptures we gain hope. Let us see how this encouragement and hope have come to the lives of other Christians through the Scriptures and can come to our lives today.

The Rod and Staff of Scripture

Henry Van Dyke says, "The Bible comes into the palace to tell the monarch that he is a servant of the Most High, and into the cottage to assure the peasant that he is a son of God! Children listen to its stories with wonder and delight, and wise men ponder them as parables of life. The Bible has a word of peace for the time of peril, and a word of light for the hour of darkness. The wicked and the proud tremble at its warnings, but to the wounded and penitent it has a mother's voice. It has woven itself into our deepest dreams so that love, friendship, sympathy and devotion, memory and hope put on the beautiful garments of its treasured speech, breathing its frankincense and myrrh. No man is poor or desolate who has this treasure for his own. When the landscape darkens and the trembling pilgrim comes to the valley of the shadow, he is not afraid to enter. He takes the rod and staff of Scripture in his hand and says to his friends and comrades, 'Goodby, we shall meet again.' Comforted by that support, he walks through momentary darkness into eternal light."

St. Seraphim of Sarov

St. Seraphim of Sarov found encouragement and hope daily in the Scriptures:

" . . . And I, humble Seraphim," said the starets, "for this reason go through the Gospel daily. On Monday I read St. Matthew from beginning to end. On Tuesday, St. Mark; on Wednesday, St. Luke; on Thursday, St. John; the other days I divide between the Acts of the Apostles and the Epistles of the Apostles. And I do not for a single day neglect to read the daily Epistle and Gospel, and also the readings to the saints. Through this not only my soul but also my body rejoices and is vivified. Because I converse with the Lord I hold in my mind His Life and Suffering, and day and night I glorify and give thanks to my Redeemer for all His mercies that are shed upon mankind and upon me, the unworthy one."

He added elsewhere: "A man's mind must swim in the Scriptures."

St. Chrysostom

St. John Chrysostom wrote:

"Listen, those of you who are living in the world

(that is, not clergy or monks) and have a wife and children; how to you also St. Paul commits especially the readings of Scripture (when he says, 'Let the Word of Christ dwell in you richly in all wisdom.' Colossians 3:16); and that not to be done lightly, nor in any sort of way, but with much earnestness. Listen, I entreat you, all that are careful for the Christian life and procure books that will be medicines for the soul. If you will not get any others, get at least the New Testament, the Epistles, the Acts, the Gospels for your constant teachers. If grief befalls you, dive into them as into a chest of medicine, and take comfort from them in your troubles, be it loss, or death, or bereavement . . . or rather do not just dive into them, but take them wholly into yourself, keep them in your mind. *For this is the cause of all evils: not knowing the Scriptures*" (Homily IX on Colossians).

Encouragement in Death

A person tells of the encouragement received from Scripture at the death of his father:

"Father had been sick a long time, and his sickness at last proved fatal. In the family were four children of whom I, the eldest, was only twelve.

"I shall never forget the shock we children felt when mother told us that father had died. We all cried as though our hearts would break.

"Then mother did something which has been a source of comfort and peace to me throughout all the years that have followed. She sat down in her rocking chair and gathered us children around her.

"Opening the Bible she read to us those immortal words of our Savior: 'Let not your heart be troubled . . . I will not leave you comfortless . . . Peace I leave with you, my peace I give unto you: not as the world giveth, give I unto you. Let not your heart be troubled, neither let it be afraid.' Then she commended each of us to God in prayer.

"Our crying stopped, and there came upon us the 'peace of God, which passeth all understanding.' "

By the encouragement of the Scriptures this family gained hope!

Case Histories

The great Russian novelist Dostoevsky spent four years in a prison camp in Siberia. While there, he went through what he called, "unspeakable, interminable suffering." The only thing that provided the comfort and strength he needed to survive was a small New Testament two Christian women had given him on his way to Siberia. It kept him from going to pieces. *By the encouragement of the Scriptures he gained hope!*

A woman was facing a serious operation. She was frightened even though she knew she had the best doctors and many friends praying for her. Her pastor did his best to comfort her but she was still too frightened for the operation. Then, lying alone in bed one night in the hospital, she opened the Bible and read the Psalms—all of them. A few days later, following surgery, she said to her pastor, "You know, I read all the Psalms the night before my operation. I don't remember a word I read, but I received the strong conviction that God was real and was with me, and my fear vanished." *By the encouragement of the Scriptures she gained hope!*

A young socialite, married to a rich contractor, felt a deep emptiness in her life. Nothing pleased her. She took to drinking. Her marriage was on the verge of divorce. Musing one day that psychiatrists had been no help, she impulsively purchased a Bible and began reading it. After reading right through the night, she suddenly felt what she later described as "the most marvelous feeling of peace and release." Her emptiness was filled by God. She and her husband became changed persons. *By the encouragement of the Scriptures she gained hope!*

What Encouragement!

Listen to some of the encouragement God gives us through the Scriptures:

"God so loved the world that he gave his only Son, that whoever believes in him should not perish but have eternal life" (John 3:16).

The encouragement of God's love!

"My sheep hear my voice, and I know them, and they follow me; and I give them eternal life, and they shall never perish, and no one shall snatch them out of my hand" (John 10:27-28).

The encouragement of eternal security in Christ!

"Have no anxiety about anything, but in everything by prayer and supplication with thanksgiving let your requests be made known to God. And the peace of God, which passes all understanding, will keep your hearts and minds in Chist Jesus" (Phil. 4:6-7).

The encouragement of God's loving care and provision for each one of us!

Ambrose of Milan said, "As in Paradise, God walks in the Holy Scriptures, seeking man." Open the Scriptures daily and let God find you. He is walking there seeking to find you, to give you encouragement and hope!

"Whatever was written in former days was written

for our instruction, that . . . by the encouragement of the Scriptures we might have hope."

PRAYER

Thank You, Lord, for the Bible which is a door leading to your presence. But a door, if it is not opened, is just another part of the wall. Help me to open the Scriptures daily to find there your presence which is constantly seeking me. Amen.

I Belong to Christ

Eighth Sunday of Matthew (I Corinthians 1:10-17)

"What I mean is that each one of you says: 'I belong to Paul,' or 'I belong to Apollos,' or 'I belong to Cephas,' or 'I belong to Christ'" (I Cor. 1:12).

One night during the First World War a chaplain crawled through the trenches. He came upon a dying, agonizing soldier. He tried to help him; took his torn, bleeding body into his arms and whispered words of spiritual help and consolation to him. The boy opened his eyes and looked somewhat startled at the priest. "Father," he gasped, "I do not belong to your Church." The chaplain answered, "I know, my lad, but you belong to my God."

The Need to Belong

According to modern psychology there are three basic needs in man: the need to have significance, the need to have security, and the need to belong. The strongest and most basic is the need to belong.

This is why everyone, no matter how old or how young, wants to belong. We like to feel we belong to a family, a club, a country. We have all kinds of clubs for people to join: clubs for tall people, short people, single people, married people, old people, young people. Belonging is a basic psychological need. It makes people feel that they are wanted, loved, needed, appreciated.

In the motion picture "West Side Story" a boy sings of what it means to belong to the Jets, a neighborhood gang. When you belong to the Jets "you're never disconnected, you always walk by two's, by three's, by four's."

Why This Need?

Why does man have such an instinctive, irrepressible need to belong? What makes him that way? There is only one real answer. God made him that way. The Bible tells us that God made man in His own image. That means that man was created to belong to God! He was made with a capacity to know, love, and have fellowship with God. Man's need to belong is at bottom a need to belong to God. At its deepest level that need to belong is met by the Church in a way that cannot be matched by any clan, group or club. We belong to God and God's family. Every other level of belonging is transitory, bound to this earth. Belonging to Christ binds us together in the eternal family of God.

Man's loneliness and isolation, his sense of not belonging, is due to the fact that he has separated himself from God through sin. Here lies the meaning of what God did for us in Christ, Who came to earth and suffered on the Cross to bring us back to God, to Whom we belong. Christ is the bridge between man and God. He is the One Who restores the broken relationship to God. He opens the door to communion with God. "God was in Christ reconciling the world to Himself," says St. Paul.

Paul castigates the Corinthians in today's Epistle lesson for breaking up the church into cliques that separated Christians one from the other: "I belong to Paul," said one, "I belong to Apollos," said another. "I belong to Cephas," said still another. Then Paul comes in strong to make his point: "But I belong to Christ! Is Christ divided? Was Paul crucified for you? Or were you baptized in the name of Paul?" (I Cor. 1:12-13). We belong to Christ!

"Twice Mine!"

There is a story of a boy who worked long tedious hours making a model ship. When it was finished he delighted in sailing it along the river. One day he left the little boat tied to a tree along the river bank and returned to find it gone. He was very sad because he treasured the little craft, particularly since he had made it with his own hands.

Not long afterward he passed a store window and to his great surprise saw there his own boat marked, "For Sale."

Overjoyed he bolted into the store and told the owner about the boat on display. It really belonged to him. He had made it with his own hands.

"I'm sorry," said the storekeeper, "but it's *my* boat now. If you want it, you'll have to pay the price for it."

The boy asked to have the boat put aside for him and went out to earn money to buy it back. Later, with his precious boat under his arms, he told the storekeeper, "Now it's twice mine—mine because I made it—and now, mine because I bought it."

If the message of the cross has anything to say to us it is this: we belong to God. We are His not once but twice: first because He made us, and second because when we sold ourselves to sin, He wanted us so greatly that He paid the price to buy us back. The price was tremendous—the highest price that could ever be paid. It was the sacrifice of His own Son, Jesus, upon the Cross of Calvary. "You know that you were ransomed," writes St. Peter, "not with perishable things such as silver and gold, but with the precious blood of Christ . . . " (I Peter 1:18). And because of this *we belong to Him.* Today. Tomorrow. Throughout eternity.

Branded!

As ranchers brand their cattle, as ancient Romans branded their slaves, so God brands us as His very own through baptism. The mark of baptism and chrismation sets us apart as belonging to God.

The story is told of a Russian officer who was captured by Napoleon's men. He was brought into the emperor's presence. The branding iron was applied to the palm of his hand. He gritted his teeth and stood unflinchingly as the letter "N" was burned into the sizzling flesh. When he asked the meaning of this he was told that he was now the property of the great Napoleon. Instantly he drew his sword and cut off his branded hand. His defiant reply was, "I belong body, soul and mind to the Czar of Russia!"

It is no Czar but God who deserves this kind of loyalty. When the world tries to brand us with its sin, we can stand as staunch soldiers of God and say, as Joseph did when he was tempted to sin, "I cannot yield to this sin. I won't, for I belong to God."

A person who was wallowing in the gutter of sin said to his pastor: "I know I'm in the gutter. I *know* it. But, oh, I don't belong there, do I? Tell me, I don't belong there!"

The pastor put his arm around him and said, "No, you don't belong there. You belong to Him who loved you enough to forsake the courts of heaven and die on the cross for you. You belong to the Crucified Christ who said to the penitent thief, 'Today you will be with me in paradise.' You belong to heaven."

Identity Crisis

We are told that man today is suffering an identity crisis; he does not know who he is. Man will never know who he is until he meets Jesus at the Cross. It is there that man comes to realize his true identity: that he is loved by God, that he belongs to God, that he is worth to God as much as the blood of His only Son. "Now we are the sons of God, and it does not yet appear what we shall be." This is who we are. "I have not called you servants," said Jesus to His disciples, "I have called you friends." Man will never know who he is until he comes to see himself as belonging to God in love. A mother said to her son who was about to leave home to settle in a foreign country: "John, always remember whose son you are." Our heavenly Father speaks these same words to each one of us: "Remember whose son or daughter you are."

Scripture

How cogently the word of God in Scripture speaks of our belonging to God. St. Paul writes: "If we live, we live to the Lord, and if we die, we die to the Lord; so then, whether we live or whether we die, we are the Lord's" (Romans 14:8). In the story of the ninety-nine sheep, the Good Shepherd—Jesus—leaves the ninety-nine sheep in the fold to go out and search for the one that was lost. He could not rest as long as that one sheep was away from him! This is how seriously he considers our belonging to him. To show that we belong to God in death as well as in life, Jesus' last words were: "Father, into your hands I commend my spirit." In Matthew 23:37 Jesus said, "O Jerusalem, Jerusalem, killing the prophets and stoning those who are sent to you! How often would I have gathered your children together as a hen gathers her brood under her wings, and you would not!" "Under His wings"—this is where every commited Christian belongs!

Practical Implications

The practical implications of our belonging to God are many.

1. We often hear it said that a person can do what he likes with his own body. This is brought up especially when talking of illicit sex and abortion. St. Paul tells us that this is simply not true for the Christian. Our body is not our own. It belongs to God. A price has been paid for it. It is God's temple, and it has to be kept holy for Him. "Don't you know," he says, "that your body is a temple of the Holy Spirit? You are not your own. You were purchased with a price. Therefore glorify God in your body."

2. Most dogs love to run after kittens. Not so the seeing-eye dog. He goes right on his way undistracted. He knows his master and will let nothing interfere with his service to him. So it is with the Christian who knows he belongs to Christ. Truly commited to one Master, he does not chase after everything that comes along. He

knows who he is, to whom he belongs, and where he is going.

3. If I belong to God, then I am His property. When the devil comes to tempt me I have the right to say to him, "Take your hands off me. I do not belong to you. I am God's property!"

4. When we truly belong to Christ then we belong to each other. For then we become members of the same body—the Body of Christ. Being members of the same body, we rely on each other for sustenance and support. This is why Jesus just before He expired, entrusted the care of His mother to the Apostle John, "Behold, your mother," He said to him. Only when men truly belong to God can they truly belong to one another.

5. Because we belong to Christ, nothing—not even death—can ever separate us from Him, "For I am persuaded," said St. Paul, "that neither death, nor life, nor angels, nor principalities, nor powers, nor things present, nor things to come, nor height, nor depth, nor any other creature, shall be able to separate us from the love of God, which is in Christ Jesus our Lord" (Romans 8:38-39). Is not this, life's greatest security: to know that we belong to Christ and that nothing can ever separate us from Him?

A devoted missionary to India, facing death by cancer said, "I don't belong to death, I belong to Christ. I was never so happy as I am right now." When we belong to the Crucified and Risen Christ, everything belongs to us: victory over death, deliverance from sin, eternal life.

PRAYER

Lord, all that You did for me on the Cross tells me

that my life is not my own. By Your death and resurrection You made me Your very own. Help me to live under Your direction, always ready to hear the call, "Follow me"; always aware of Your presence; always living so that others may receive Your love and mercy through me. Take the whole of me, Lord, every bit of me and let me work for You, for I belong altogether to You. Amen.